from conservation to ecology: the development of environmental concern

from conservation to ecology: the development of environmental concern

EDITED BY CARROLL PURSELL

University of California, Santa Barbara

problem studies in american history

Thomas Y. Crowell Company
New York
Established 1834

Library of Congress Cataloging in Publication Data

PURSELL, CARROLL W., ed.
    From conservation to ecology.

    CONTENTS: Nash, R. The American
democracy: the conservation movement.—Bates,
J. L. Fulfilling American democracy: the
conservation movement.—Hays, S. P. The
conservation movement and the progressive
tradition. [etc.]

    1. Environmental policy—United States
—Addresses, essays, lectures. 2. Ecology—United
States—Addresses, essays, lectures. 3. Natural
resources—United States—Addresses, essays,
lectures. I. Title.
HC110.E5P87   301.31′0973   72-10945
ISBN 0-690-31805-7

The frontispiece cartoon is from Environmental
Action 2, no. 1 (14 May 1970): 6–7. *Reprinted by
permission, Sawyer Press, Los Angeles, Calif.
90046, U.S.A.*

Manufactured in the United States of America

1 2 3 4 5 6 7 8 9 10

preface

The purpose of this volume is to present a narrative account (necessarily somewhat episodic) of the development of American concern for the environment. The organization is largely chronological, moving from the wilderness through the first conservation crusade of the early twentieth century to the rediscovery of the environmental problems in the post-World War II era.

The major controversy among historians in this area is over the nature of that first conservation movement—did its "progressive" nature grow out of its democratic rhetoric or out of its bureaucratic practice? Although subsequent events, men, and movements are not without controversy, this controversy is more polemical than scholarly. Historians have hardly begun to study the later period, and in the meantime we can merely indicate some of those points that are likely to be disputed.

Finally, although values are not ignored completely, the emphasis here is upon public policy. The popular Pogoism that "we have met the enemy and his is us" is much too simple and misleading an analysis of the crisis that faces America. Like racism, ecocide may well grow out of values—but it certainly manifests itself in policies and their institutional embodiments.

Carroll Pursell

contents

INTRODUCTION   1

1. The American Wilderness
in Historical Perspective   7
Roderick Nash

2. Fulfilling American Democracy:
The Conservation Movement   20
James Leonard Bates

3. The Conservation Movement and the Progressive
Tradition   37
Samuel P. Hays

4. *from* Federal Conservation Policy, 1921–1933   48
Donald C. Swain

5. Conservation in 1952   58
Stephen Raushenbush

6. *from* Silent Spring   69
Rachel Carson

7. Can We Survive?   79
Barry Commoner

8. American Institutions and Ecological Ideals   90
Leo Marx

9. Ecological Armageddon   106
Robert Heilbroner

10. The Profits in Pollution   116
Ralph Nader

11. The Eco-Establishment   122
Katherine Barkley and Steve Weissman

12. Black Ecology   130
Nathan Hare

13. Perilous Links between Economic Growth, Justice and Ecology:
A Challenge for Economic Planners   137
Norman J. Faramelli

SELECTED BIBLIOGRAPHY   145

from conservation to ecology: the development of environmental concern

introduction

A Gallup Poll published in the spring of 1970 documented
the obvious fact that the environment and its degradation
had rapidly become a political issue of major dimensions.
Since the mid-nineteen-sixties, the proportion of Americans
identifying "reducing pollution of air and water" as
one of the three most pressing problems of government
had risen from 17 to 53 percent. Twice before in this
century—during the Progressive Era and during the
Depression—crusades to conserve the nation's natural
resources had crested and then receded. Like other national
concerns, that for the environment varied with the times.

The problem had been a long time building. In 1831
the English novelist Frances Trollope was traveling down
the Mohawk Valley of New York, recently opened to
new commerce by the Erie Canal. A Yankee with her
party apologized for the "wild state of the country" and
blamed it on the fact that until recently it had been owned
by an Englishman. "When the English gets a spot of
wild ground like this here," he explained, "they have no
notions about it like us; but . . . if you was to see it five
years hence, you would not know it again; I'll engage
there will be by that, half a score elegant factories—'tis true
shame to let such a privilege of water lie idle."

The Yankee had behind him already two centuries of
concern for growth and development. For all those two
hundred years the goal had been to tame the wild, to
civilize the savage, and to make productive the howling
waste. It was not only a moral imperative but also an
economic necessity if the American dream was to be realized.
Vigorous exploitation of the continent's natural resources
would result in economic growth sufficient to insure
prosperity and independence for all Americans. Our
liberties, our welfare, and our immortal souls were all
dependent upon growth and exploitation.

By the end of the nineteenth century the frontier had
closed, manufacturing had surpassed agriculture as our
most important industry, and our cities were burgeoning
and filling with increasingly strange and vaguely dangerous
foreigners. Abroad, we continued our territorial expansion
in the Caribbean and the far Pacific. At home, the
business elite and the new urban middle class combined
to rationalize society—to bring order out of our chaotic
inheritance of unrestricted individualism and localism.

1

During the Progressive Era the eminently rational ideals of "conservation" and "efficiency" spawned reforms in a multitude of problem areas, not the least of which was the hitherto prodigal disposition of the nation's natural resources.

The history of the American wilderness clearly demonstrates a clash of values. Roderick Nash reminds us that the early frontiersmen set about to tame the alien wilderness under the Biblical sanction of Genesis 1:28: ". . . replenish the earth, and subdue it: and have dominion over . . . every living thing that moveth upon the earth." Yet there has always been a subtle ambivalence in man's attitude toward the wilderness—one that made even Daniel Boone pause briefly in his career of exploration and settlement. Throughout the nineteenth century, and into our own, an increasing number of "preservationists" have made some gains in saving bits of the wilderness for posterity. Not all joined John Muir in considering them sacred groves, but even the idea that they were available for "a higher use" at least kept them from other forms of exploitation. The wilderness movement was critical in extending the list of values that Americans could find acceptable.

The major thrust of public policy on resource questions after 1900 was not determined by the preservationists, despite such victories as the establishment of the National Park Service in 1916. Those who shaped the new resource policy of the Progressive Era were called conservationists, and the name accurately defined their purpose—to prevent waste through efficient utilization. Led by the chief forester Gifford Pinchot, the conservationists won Theodore Roosevelt to their cause and made their concern one of the major forces of his administration. J. Leonard Bates has given us an appealing picture of these men, who had a "fighting, democratic faith" and a policy based on "limited socialism in the public interest." It was a view thoroughly consistent with the traditional picture of progressivism itself as a movement of the people struggling to wrest control of the nation from powerful special interests. Looking back at our first conservation crusade, Bates finds it "an effort to implement democracy for twentieth-century America, to stop the stealing and exploitation, to inspire high standards of government, to preserve the beauty of mountain and stream, to distribute more equitably the profits of this economy."

The conservation movement described by Samuel P. Hays was quite a different thing. A pioneering effort in the revision of historical thinking about progressivism, his book *Conservation and the Gospel of Efficiency* (1959) emphasized not Bates's "fighting, democratic faith" but rather "the application of the new technology to resource management." Grass-roots democracy, for the conservationists, would "defeat the inner spirit of the gospel of efficiency. Indeed, experts, using technical and scientific methods, should decide all matters of development and utilization of resources, all problems of allocation of funds." Roosevelt was attracted to the movement in large part because conservation was an issue that he hoped would not raise fundamental social questions. Like Richard Nixon in 1970, Roosevelt realized that the balm of disinterested expertise could soothe the angry wounds of social conflict.

In the traditional view, conservation, like progressivism generally, subsided during the 1920s until recalled to life by the idealism and social reform of

Franklin D. Roosevelt's New Deal. As Donald C. Swain shows, the lack
of strong charismatic presidents dedicated to crusading resource policies
disappointed some conservationists, but the expertise and bureaucratic nature
of the progressive movement lived on in the federal agencies. Indeed, in this as in
so many respects, the administration of Herbert Hoover served as a logical
introduction to that of Franklin D. Roosevelt.

It has been said that resource policy was the one clear and consistent line of
development in the New Deal. Whatever other faults he had as a policy
maker, Roosevelt was a firm advocate of resource planning and conservation.
Through commemorative postage stamps and fireside chats, from the Tennessee
Valley Authority to the National Resources Board, he gave his impressive backing
to the idea that the nation's natural resources were for the benefit of all the
people of the nation, and that their interrelations should be studied and
respected in planning for their use. During the 1930s young men from
the Civilian Conservation Corps (CCC) and the Soil Conservation Service,
the Biological Survey, and the Fish and Wildlife Service, symbolized the
activism and concern of the New Deal. By the outbreak of World War II it was
possible to believe that the waste of our natural resources, like the waste
of our human resources—both so strongly deplored by an able and popular
president—had been averted.

Slowly during the 1950s the nation began to realize that many of the ghosts
of social disaster, thought to have been laid forever by the New Deal, were
still abroad in the land. Poverty was rediscovered, race relations were found to be
little improved, and it was gradually realized that the position of women in
American society was actually deteriorating. Mutual security had failed to
provide national security, and at home corporate greed and irresponsibility
were found again in all their classic guises. In 1952 Stephen Raushenbush
took a dim view of the state of conservation in the nation. He carefully identified
the factors that had muffled the impulse of previous years, and catalogued the
unmet needs. Perhaps most importantly, he illuminated the "interesting but
controversial concept that the ultimate function of all the raw materials
in the world is that of supporting the high American standard of living." The
search for raw materials abroad was intimately intertwined with the success
of conservation at home. By way of solution he could only hope that
technical expertise would develop the true facts of our situation and that a
new conservation movement would spring from these.

As it happened the movement was begun not by the experts but by a
nature writer whom the experts tried vainly to discredit. First in a series of
articles in the magazine *The New Yorker,* and then in her brilliantly successful
book *Silent Spring* (1962), Rachel Carson spotlighted the disastrous side
effects of the massive use of chemical pesticides. One of the prides and successes
of agricultural science, the pesticides, especially DDT, had found increasing
use since World War II. The evolution of farming technology and consumer
tastes, coupled with soil exhaustion and a rapidly increasing population,
had placed a premium on techniques which would vastly increase crop yields.
Rachel Carson was careful to recognize this need, but she was movingly
eloquent in her denunciation of the failure to monitor and control "side effects"

properly. In the best tradition of crusading journalism, her book jolted a nation grown complacent in its violation of the environment.

The environmental movement that began to gather momentum during the 1960s was more than simply a revival of Pinchot's conservationism, or even of a new fusion of this with John Muir's preservationism. As Michael McClowskey, executive director of the Sierra Club, has pointed out, the new movement is not yet clear in outline or potential. Its components reach far beyond the old alliances to include, as McClowskey says, "the consumer movement, including the corporate reformers; the movement for scientific responsibility; a revitalized public health movement; birth control and population stabilization groups; pacifists and those who stress participatory democracy in which decisions are made consensually; young people who emphasize direct action; and a diffuse movement in search of a new focus for politics." It is a rich and unstable mixture, despite the salve of corporate liberalism and political opportunism so lavished upon it.

The scientific responsibility wing is well represented in the writings of Dr. Barry Commoner. It has long been a truism that what affects California, affects the nation, and that what affects the United States, eventually shall shake the world. If the future of mankind is written already on the California landscape, then, as Commoner demonstrates, we are in perilous straits indeed. Essentially, he makes an appeal from science drunk to science sober—the "wisdom of science" and the "power of technology" should be directed to "the welfare, the survival of man."

Just as environmental irresponsibility has lain close to the center of Western civilization from the time our forefathers sought dominion over their environment, so has a basic ecological attitude long been invoked as a fundamental critique of that civilization. Leo Marx has pointed out that some of the best and most sensitive American writers of the nineteenth century saw clearly that our rampaging industrial capitalism, which was almost universally applauded as a good thing, was in fact fatally destructive of life and understanding. The current convergence of insights, as he calls it, from science and literature promises a new strength and vigor not only for efforts to "save the environment," but also for a true reformation of values and reform of institutions.

It has long been realized that growth, as such, is one of the basic problems of society—growth both of our population and of the economy. The writings of Paul Ehrlich combine several of the themes of the new environmental movement—science responsibility for one, and most obviously the concern for overpopulation for another. Indeed he is probably the dean of the so-called neo-Malthusians. It is easier to find a biologist worried about population growth, however, than to find an economist worried about the dangers of economic growth. Robert L. Heilbroner chose to turn a review of Paul and Anne Ehrlich's book *Population, Resources, Environment* (1970) into a vehicle for describing the economic dangers of our present policies and commitments.

The movements for consumer protection and corporate responsibility are personified by Ralph Nader, the most prominent of the new public-service lawyers. Beginning with his exposé of automobile safety hazards, *Unsafe at*

Any Speed (1965), he has broadened his attack on public health hazards
and corporate irresponsibility. As in Pinchot's day, liberal corporation executives
have recently put themselves in the forefront of the environmental movement.
Firms that pollute for profit now spin off subsidiaries that make another
profit from cleaning up the pollution, and the parent organization can adopt
the new devices and procedures while passing the expense on to the public in the
form of higher prices and tax write-offs. Nader strongly attacks this
"businesslike" approach to environmental problems and suggests ways of
bringing countervailing institutions into play.

The challenge and response follow a historic symmetry. Progressive
muckrakers and the following generation of historians tended to deplore
specific corporate abuses or the general lack of responsibility on the part of big
business. Recent revisionists have found in the period not simply a battle
between the interests and the people, but more importantly a successful
effort by the corporations to define the very terms of the problem. Regulation
is now seen not primarily as a curbing of corporate power by the people,
but more importantly as a device by which corporations use the power of the
government to rationalize their business environment. Katherine Barkley and
Steve Weissman have traced the evolution of what they call the "Eco-
Establishment"—a network of public-spirited, corporate-sponsored organizations
which are attempting to update the concerns and techniques of the first
conservation crusade to meet the needs of business in the present environmental
crisis.

The same 1970 Gallup Poll that indicated a growing concern for the
problem of air and water pollution also showed another significant variation:
black Americans did not share this new concern to the same extent. While
Caucasians listed crime, pollution, and education as the greatest problems, in that
order, black Americans listed slum housing, poverty, and discrimination.
The poll served to remind us that a concern for the natural environment varies
not only through time, but also among different social groups. Nathan Hare
has contributed a sober and timely warning that the needs and preoccupations
of the white middle class and corporate elite in America are not necessarily
those which will best serve the needs of black Americans. Studies have shown
that in New York City perhaps 25,000 slum children suffer from lead
poisoning—and although "only" 5 percent die, 25 percent suffer permanent
brain damage. Nationwide, probably 225,000 children, mostly from the inner
cities, suffer from this poisoning. In California one study found that black
people carry twice as much DDT in their bodies as Caucasians. Lead on the
walls is as bad as lead in the air, and DDT in people is as alarming as
DDT in pelicans. National parks have no meaning for the poor who never
leave their own neighborhoods, let alone the cities in which they are trapped.

Hare's description of "Black Ecology" should bring us back to the most basic
principle of the new movement—that we are all caught up in a delicate
and interconnected social system. If we are not *all* served, none of us shall
be saved. Broadly interpreted, the concept of "Spaceship Earth" should remind
us of our relationship to *all* the environment, not the least of which is the
rest of mankind.

As Norman J. Faramelli reminds us, "the rest of mankind" raises the inescapable fact that as things now stand the United States, with only 5 percent of the world's population, consumes perhaps half of the world's resources. Such inequality, which tends to fall hardest on the Third World, can only cause increasing problems in the future. At home too, the patterns of consumption are wildly uneven. Large numbers of Americans get only a very small share of the nation's goods: their hope for a better life lies primarily in economic growth since redistribution appears politically unlikely. The question then remains, if a livable environment (and social justice on a global scale) demands an end to economic growth, are most Americans willing to share their limited resources with that one-third of the nation which today, as in the time of Franklin D. Roosevelt, is still "ill-housed, ill-clad, ill-nourished."

one
the american wilderness in historical perspective

RODERICK NASH

A student of American intellectual history and an ardent
outdoorsman and conservation activist, Roderick Nash
(b. 1939) here traces the evolution of American attitudes
toward their most obvious resource, a wilderness so vast
and rich as to inspire both promise and dread. The
author of The Wilderness and the American Mind *(1967),*
Nash earned his Ph.D. at the University of Wisconsin
and now teaches intellectual and environmental history
at the University of California, Santa Barbara.

Americans have found it difficult to be indifferent to a factor
so basic in their collective experience as the wilderness.
Over the years it has been regarded both as an enemy to
be conquered in the name of civilization, Christianity
and progress and as something of value to be cherished
and preserved. Today what remains of the American
wilderness is being weighed in the balance of public
judgment. Part of this evaluation involves an assessment of
the meaning of wilderness in American life which, in
turn, demands the hindsight of history.

The first settlers arrived in the New World with ideas
and intentions totally incompatible with appreciating
wilderness. They came either to squeeze a quick fortune

Source: Roderick Nash, "The American Wilderness in Historical
Perspective," *Forest History* 6 (Winter 1963): 3–13. Reprinted by
permission of the author and the publisher.

from the virgin continent or to create in it an exemplary Christian community. Nothing in their experience as Europeans prepared them for what they found. Understandably, they agreed with the Pilgrim chronicler William Bradford who reported in 1620 that there was nothing to see in New England "but a hideous and desolate wilderness, full of wild beasts and wild men—and what multitudes there might be of them they knew not." The paramount concern of the colonists was to keep the candle of civilization flickering on the edge of moral and physical darkness. Frequently the pioneers expressed their relation to the wilderness with a military metaphor: wild country was an "enemy" to be "conquered," "subdued" or "vanquished" by a "pioneer army." Any qualms the frontiersman may have felt about the propriety of invading and exploiting the wilderness were calmed with the aid of the first commandment of God to man, Genesis 1:28: "Be fruitful, and multiply, and replenish the earth, and subdue it: and have dominion over . . . every living thing that moveth upon the earth." Here was a God-given sanction to destroy the wilderness for man's benefit.

The pioneer of the colonial period shared with his 19th-century counterpart a hunger for land—agriculturally productive land. The forest wilderness was the most formidable barrier standing between him and success. He devoted his brawn and brain to the task of destroying trees. In some areas it required two months for one man to clear a single acre. Sometimes "girdling" was employed to kill a tree by cutting away a strip of bark near its base. An alternative method, as an Ohio pioneer described it, was first to fell a tree with axes: "When fairly down they went to work in dismembering it. In the meantime another party with spades dug a deep pit alongside the trunk, into which it was rolled and covered with earth, while the top and branches were thrown into heaps and burnt." As the gloom of the forest receded and light poured into the clearing, the spirits of the pioneer and his family rose. In their eyes the only good tree was a dead one in a fence, cabin wall or fireplace. Such a utilitarian value system, which in John Muir's phrase regarded trees as "pernicious weeds," had no place for wilderness. Indeed, the conquest of wild country gave meaning and purpose to pioneer existence. In his own lifetime the frontiersman could witness the radical changes which civilization wrought. If not he himself, then surely his children and grandchildren would reap the benefits of his war against wilderness. Describing the satisfactions of pioneering, one guidebook for settlers declared: "You look around and whisper, 'I vanquished this wilderness and made the chaos pregnant with order and civilization, alone I did it.' "

While the nation as a whole was trampling the continent in a march to progress and "Manifest Destiny," a few individuals recognized in a quiet corner of their minds a love of wilderness. This awareness of value in wild country other than as raw material for future economic use was a necessary prelude to the idea and achievement of wilderness preservation. The "father" of wilderness preservation in the United States was, in fact, the first nameless pioneer who momentarily lowered his axe and gazed westward from a hardwood ridge at the wild country beyond with a feeling of awe, admiration and excitement. One of the first known records of such an occurrence was in the alleged autobiography of Daniel Boone written for him by John Filson. On the one hand Boone recognized that he and his kind were the cutting edge of civilization, "an instrument ordained to settle the wilderness." But parts of the account of Boone's first experiences in the wilds of Kentucky have a different flavor:

Just at the close of day the gentle gales retired, and left the place to the disposal of a profound calm. I had gained the summit of a commanding ridge, and looking round with astonishing delight, beheld the ample plains, the beauteous tracts below. . . . At a vast distance I beheld the mountains lift their venerable brows, and penetrate the clouds.

Later Boone stated explicitly that "no populous city . . . could afford so much pleasure to my mind, as the beauties of nature I found here."

The same duality in attitude toward wilderness evident in Boone's autobiography appeared in the thought of James Hall, the literary voice of the West in the first half of the 19th century. In 1836 Hall applauded the process whereby "a savage wilderness, resting in primeval solitude . . . is suddenly opened to an eager multitude, who . . . cover it with civilized life." But he also admitted: "I know nothing more splendid than a forest of the west, standing in its original integrity, adorned with the exuberant beauties of a powerful vegetation, and crowned with the honors of a venerable age." Hall was an interesting transition figure in the growth of American appreciation of wilderness and a harbinger of things to come. The incompatibility of a wild forest and a flourishing civilization did not deter him from approving of both simultaneously.

That the Divine Being was somehow manifested in the natural world was an ancient idea dating to the dim beginnings of recorded history. In the American setting it was an important factor in promoting an appreciation of wild country. The purity of the wilderness, uncorrupted by man's artificial constructions, seemed to some Americans the ideal medium for the perception and worship of God. A New England clergyman, for example, who in 1803 crossed the Allegheny Mountains and floated down the Ohio admitted that the contemplation of a farming scene was "pleasant recreation" but declared that amidst "the majestic features of the uncultivated wilderness . . . we convene with GOD." Similar ideas of Ralph Waldo Emerson exerted a profound effect on the attitude of many of his countrymen toward the natural world. In the language of the Transcendentalists, nature was the symbol of the spiritual world and the container of moral truths which permeated the universe. Man, through his power of intuition, could discern the spiritual reality which lay behind natural objects. Under wilderness conditions it was possible for the human soul to commune most freely with the Oversoul. "In the woods," as Emerson put it, "we return to reason and faith." Ideas such as these suggested a non-utilitarian value for wilderness.

The studies of a host of American scientists, both before and after the Revolution, were another factor in stimulating appreciation of wild country. The hope of discovering new species lured men like John Bartram, the Michaux, Thomas Say and Thomas Nuttall far into the wilderness. In 1819 Nuttall expressed his reflections:

*To me the hardships and privations are cheaply purchased if I may but
roam over the wild domain of primeval nature. . . . My chief converse
has been in the wilderness with the spontaneous productions of
nature, and the study of these subjects and their contemplation
have been to me a source of constant delight.*

The work of scientists such as Nuttall encouraged others to regard wilderness
not only as potential lumber, iron ore and farmland, but as a vast laboratory
where fascinating and important facts awaited discovery. In particular the
ornithological studies of Alexander Wilson and John James Audubon did much
to spread the notion that there was beauty in living, wild subjects.

Those who came in contact with the American wilderness reacted to it as
individuals, never in fixed categories. Some like Josiah Gregg, the Santa Fe
trader of the 1830's, prized the freedom of the unfenced prairie and felt
uncomfortably constricted in civilization. For a New York journalist who enjoyed
camping trips in the Adirondack region of his state, wilderness offered the
opportunity to "talk and think as a natural, and not an artificial man." At the
conclusion of his 1857 account of sporting adventures he pleaded: "Give a
month to the enjoyment of wilderness-life, and you will return to your
labors invigorated in strength, buoyant in spirit—a wiser, healthier, and a better
man." One individual who followed this formula was Henry David Thoreau,
whose voice was one of the strongest raised in the 19th century in defense
of wilderness. From his experiences at Walden Pond and in northern Maine,
Thoreau concluded that man's optimum condition was a balance between
wilderness and civilization. Neither alone was sufficient, but together they could
maximize man's intellectual and moral growth. While civilization might
refine art, Thoreau believed wilderness was the source of creativity. He
lamented the "war with the wilderness" which his country was waging, and
felt that in its determination to civilize every acre on the continent America was
blind to a fundamental truth:

*From the forest and wilderness come the tonics and barks which brace
mankind. Our ancestors were savages. The story of Romulus and
Remus being suckled by a wolf is not a meaningless fable. The
founders of every state which has risen to eminence have drawn their
nourishment from a similar wild source.*

Such ideas had considerable impact in the years following the Revolution
when a young America was highly conscious of the importance of making its
place in the family of nations. Writers and painters like Joel Barlow and
Thomas Cole celebrated the American wilderness as a source of national
pride and greatness. Others felt that wilderness gave their country a precious
distinctiveness, the equivalent of Europe's cultural heritage. The presence of
miles of untouched country to the west seemed to be a guarantee of American
spontaneity and innocence as opposed to the allegedly cramped and artificial
conditions in the Old World.

When in 1846 a New York businessman took an extensive canoe trip into the "wild and silent wilderness" of northern Minnesota and described his feelings toward it as "composed of delight and melancholy, of perfect confidence and tormenting fear," he was reflecting the impact of a complex body of ideas commonly labeled "Romanticism." One root of the new esteem which the Romantic impulse conferred on wilderness was a change in aesthetics which took place gradually in the 18th century. Wild, natural objects such as mountains and forests ceased being regarded as "horrible" and were deemed worthy of awe and admiration. The new aesthetic category of the "sublime" encompassed awe, terror and exaltation, and as such it was well suited to describe the reactions of those who pushed into the wilderness.

An enthusiasm for the primitive was another manifestation of Romanticism. In some cases primitivism took the form of an admiration of natural man—the "noble savage" in his wilderness setting. Others delighted in the opportunity for escape and adventure that wild country offered. A Prussian prince noted in his journal that he did not come to America to see "the gigantic strides of civilization" but rather "the rude, primitive character of the natural face of North America." This was certainly the case with George Ruxton, an English adventurer, who camped in the Rocky Mountains in the 1840's and afterwards declared, "although liable to an accusation of barbarism, I must confess that the very happiest moments of my life have been spent in the wilderness of the Far West." All the luxuries of civilized life, Ruxton admitted, could not persuade him to relinquish the freedom he found in the wilderness. The famous traveler Alexis de Tocqueville summed up the Romantic attitude when he reported that the Michigan wilderness of 1831 stimulated in him "a quiet admiration, a gentle melancholy sense, and a vague distaste for civilized life; a sort of primitive instinct that makes one think with sadness that soon this delightful solitude will have changed its looks."

The premonition Tocqueville had about the vanishing wilderness derived from an accurate assessment of the American temper. Although a few individuals found reason to value wilderness for its own sake, most still regarded it as raw material waiting and predestined to be subdued to man's use. Moreover, so vast seemed the wilderness that its complete conquest was unthinkable. Only a few had the foresight to realize that if steps were not taken to preserve parts of wild America, it would vanish. In 1832 the painter of the American Indian, George Catlin, made the first known plea for wilderness preservation. On a journey up the Missouri River, Catlin was appalled at the rapidity with which the buffalo and Indian were being exterminated. He proposed that the government preserve "in their pristine beauty and wildness, in a magnificent park, where the world could see for ages to come, the native Indian in his classic attire, galloping his wild horse . . . amid the fleeting herds of elks and buffaloes." Here was a root of the national park idea.

An area thousands of miles from the upper Missouri was the setting of the next appearance of the idea of wilderness preservation. In 1857 Samuel H. Hammond, a New York newspaper man, proposed that "a circle of a hundred miles in diameter" be set aside in his state's Adirondack region. Hammond added:

*I would make it a forest forever. It should be a misdemeanor to chop
down a tree, and a felony to clear an acre within its boundaries. The old
woods should stand here always as God made them, growing on
until the earthworm ate away their roots, and the strong winds
hurled them to the ground, and new woods should be permitted to
supply the place of the old so long as the earth remained.*

The following year Thoreau seconded Hammond's plea. He concluded a
description of a trip in the wilderness of northern Maine with the question:

*Why should not we . . . have our national preserves . . . in which the
bear and panther, and some even of the hunter race, may still exist, and
not be "civilized off the face of the earth,"—our forests, not to hold
the king's game merely, but to hold and preserve the king himself . . .
not for idle sport or food, but for inspiration and our own true
recreation? or shall we, like villains, grub them all up, poaching on
our own national domain?*

For Thoreau the ultimate end of the preservation of wilderness was the
preservation of man.

Although George Perkins Marsh's book of 1864 appeared under the title
Man and Nature, he intended it to be called *Man the Disturber of Nature's
Harmonies.* The original title was more apt because in the volume Marsh turned
his attention to the problem of man's relation to his environment in the hope
of suggesting the importance of restoring the "disturbed harmonies" that he felt
should exist between man and the natural world. Marsh advocated the
preservation of forests, arguing that the indiscriminate clearing of woods was
the prelude to floods, erosion and ultimately the collapse of civilization.
As an example he cited the consequences of the denudation of the forests of the
Roman Empire. In the second edition of his book, Marsh discussed the
"poetical" and "economical" arguments for the preservation of wilderness and
concluded:

*It is desirable that some large and easily accessible region of American
soil should remain, as far as possible, in its primitive condition, at
once a museum for the instruction of the student, a garden for the
recreation of the lover of nature, and an asylum where indigenous tree,
and humble plant . . . and fish and fowl and four-footed beast, may
dwell and perpetuate their kind. . . .*

By restoring the harmony between man and nature through wilderness
preservation, Marsh hoped to spare his country the fate of the Roman Empire
and allow it to reach lofty intellectual and artistic heights.

In 1864 California's Yosemite Valley and Mariposa Big Tree Grove were
preserved as a state park "for public use, resort, and recreation." The park
consisted of only about ten square miles, too small an area to be considered

wilderness, and it soon became the site of a large-scale tourist-catering business. But the reservation of part of the public domain for its scenic values in the name of the people laid the groundwork for the creation of a true wilderness preserve eight years later.

In 1872 over 3,500 square miles of wilderness, largely in northwestern Wyoming, were made by act of Congress the Yellowstone National Park. Although the creation of the park was the world's first act of large-scale wilderness preservation in the public interest, it was not recognized as such either by those who worked for its establishment, by Congress or by the American people. Instead Yellowstone was seen as protecting "curiosities" such as geysers and waterfalls and preventing them from falling into private hands. It was not until over a decade after its establishment, and then only occasionally, that the park was recognized and defended as a wilderness preserve. The original act creating Yellowstone was wilderness preservation in fact but not in intent.

Westward expansion left a large island of heavily forested, mountainous country in northern New York in wilderness condition. The preservation of the Adirondacks in 1885 as "wild forest lands" was the second milestone in the early history of wilderness preservation. The act of the New York legislature which set aside over 700,000 acres stemmed from the widespread conviction at the time that a forested watershed was a necessity for maintaining the vital carrying capacity of the Erie Canal and for supplying New York City with water. As the New York *Tribune* expressed it, to disturb wilderness conditions in the Adirondacks would be "tampering with the goose that lays the golden egg." Utilitarian motives governed the concern of New York for its wilderness. An untouched watershed, it was claimed, meant goods on the wharves of New York merchants and an abundance of pure water on their tables. In 1892 a state park was established in the Adirondacks, bringing the total area preserved to more than 2,000,000 acres. When a new state constitution was drafted two years later, the convention inserted a clause which made the wilderness inviolate.

In 1890, three thousand miles across the continent from the Adirondacks, another large chunk of the American wilderness was preserved in the public interest. The creation of Yosemite National Park was the third noteworthy achievement in the early history of American wilderness preservation, but the first to be undertaken with the understanding that it was *wilderness,* not geysers or a watershed, which was being protected. In large part responsible for Yosemite was a slender Scotch-American named John Muir. Arriving in California in 1868 at the age of thirty, Muir spent the following decades exploring Alaska and the American West. A gifted writer, he had a talent for describing wilderness and expounding its values as he saw them. Muir's articles beginning in the 1870's in *Century, Atlantic Monthly* and *Harper's* and his books enjoyed a circulation that put him in a class with Thoreau as a leading force in shaping American thought on the subject of wilderness. Quite simply, Muir believed that the wilderness was God's temple where His works were most clearly displayed before man. Carrying the Transcendentalist position to its extreme, Muir noted in his journal that "the clearest way into the Universe is through a forest wilderness." He pleaded with the American people to turn to the wild places of their country:

Thousands of tired, nerve-shaken, over-civilized people are beginning to find out that going to the mountains is going home; that wildness is a necessity; and that mountain parks and reservations are useful not only as fountains of timber and irrigating rivers, but as fountains of life.

In Muir's writing the "higher" uses of wilderness as a source of religion, recreation and beauty were capably defended.

The idea for a 1,600-square-mile national park surrounding the ten-square-mile Yosemite State Park of 1864 occurred to Robert Underwood Johnson, associate editor of *Century,* in 1889 while on a camping trip with John Muir in the Sierras. Together the two men launched a national campaign. Muir contributed several articles to *Century* in which he argued for Yosemite National Park on the grounds of saving "the fineness of wildness." Johnson, who managed the bill before Congressional committees, based his case for the park on its role in preserving "the beauty of nature in its wildest aspects." The brief Congressional debate was along these lines, and the act of October 1, 1890, marked the first *conscious* preservation of wilderness for its own sake in American history.

In 1892 John Muir and some California friends organized the Sierra Club for the purpose, among other things, of enlisting "the support of the people and the government in preserving the forests and other features of the Sierra Nevada Mountains." With the founding of the Sierra Club, America had its first organization dedicated to wilderness preservation, although earlier groups such as the Rocky Mountain Club (1875), the Appalachian Mountain Club (1876) and the Boone and Crockett Club (1885) could be counted on to lend support. *Forest and Stream,* the first issue of which appeared in 1873, provided an outlet for preservationist thought. The few friends of the American wilderness would need all the support they could muster because in the 1890's they found themselves increasingly at odds with a vigorous group of professional foresters under the leadership of young Gifford Pinchot.

An act of 1891 had given the President power to set aside vast acreage in the public domain as forest reserves, later called national forests. With a pen stroke, Benjamin Harrison and Grover Cleveland reserved some 34,000,000 acres of western land under this law. At first there was no policy as to how the reserved forest should be administered, but Pinchot and his followers regarded them as a crop to be scientifically cultivated for maximum sustained yield. They applied to the wilderness the same utilitarian yardstick as had the pioneers, the difference, and a significant one, being that they wished to use its resources efficiently with an eye to the needs of future Americans. Although Pinchot was not opposed to, and indeed desired, aesthetically pleasing forests, his "wise use" policy put the nation's economic welfare first.

John Muir challenged Pinchot's doctrine with his own of "right use."

To Muir's way of thinking the forest reserves should be dedicated first and foremost to wilderness preservation. His experience with lumber and grazing operations in the Sierras convinced him that even managed or scientific forestry was incompatible with the "higher" uses of wilderness. Occasionally Muir revealed a realistic appreciation of his country's need for forest products, but he felt there was already enough forest land in productive use. Consequently, Muir believed that "government protection should be thrown around every wild grove and forest on the mountains" which still remained. This position was consistent with Muir's philosophy which stressed the non-utilitarian values of wilderness.

Both the Pinchot and Muir wings of the American conservation movement, which by 1897 were in open conflict over the management of the forest reserves, were sincerely convinced that its own program had the true interests of the nation at heart. Accusing the wilderness preservationists of wishing to "lock up" natural resources, the Pinchot faction, seconded by (but by no means equated with) lumber, grazing and mining interests, obtained the ear of the McKinley administration. In 1897 they succeeded in securing by Congressional act a definition of forest management policy favorable to their "wise use" principles. With the forest reserves legally open to economic use, the national parks alone protected the American wilderness until later in the 20th century.

In spite of the split within the conservation movement in which the short end went to wilderness, the "conservation crusade" in the early years of the present century awakened many Americans to the fact of a vanishing wilderness. In this atmosphere of growing national concern about the relationship of man to land there occurred America's first major debate over the fate of a particular wilderness area: the Hetch Hetchy Valley in California's Yosemite National Park.

In 1901 the City of San Francisco, ostensibly in need of a municipal water supply but not oblivious to the profit-making potential of a cheap source of hydro-electric power, made application to the Federal government for the right to use Hetch Hetchy Valley as a reservoir. At first the city was rebuffed, the parks were to remain inviolate, but the disastrous earthquake of April, 1906, gave new urgency to San Francisco's demands. Application for Hetch Hetchy was made again, opposition formed, and the question of whether the valley should be a wilderness or a reservoir engaged Congressional committees in two sets of hearings. Newspapers and magazines gave national coverage to the controversy. John Muir and the Sierra Club worked at a fever pitch to keep Hetch Hetchy wild, appealing to Americans to protect their national park, and arguing that San Francisco had other sources of water supply available which would not destroy wilderness.

Late in 1913 Woodrow Wilson signed a Congressional act giving Hetch Hetchy to San Francisco. For John Muir, who had less than a year to live, the defeat was a bitter blow and an indication that the pioneer ethic he sought to alter with regard to wilderness still persisted. But in defeat wilderness preservation had come of age. In the Hetch Hetchy controversy, as never before, the problem of America's remaining wilderness under pressure from utilitarian demands was fully aired. National publicity generated considerable enthusiasm for wilderness in quarters hitherto unconcerned, and when San Francisco's misrepresentations were revealed, the cause gained still more friends. Like the *Maine*, "Hetch Hetchy" was remembered as a symbol in the ranks of future defenders of the wilderness.

Several factors related to changes in American civilization combined to give wilderness a new meaning in the 20th century. More people than ever before lived in large cities and the trend was upward. From the perspective of a sidewalk, wilderness lost the fearfulness and the role of formidable enemy which it had for the pioneer in a forest clearing. In fact, the elements of risk, mystery and hardship associated with wilderness which had repelled most pioneers became magnetic to many city dwellers. They joined Theodore Roosevelt in exalting the vigorous and manly qualities derived from wilderness camping. American civilization had once been a mere speck on a wild continent. With the tables turned and civilization in control, the grandchildren of the pioneers had no reason to maintain their ancestors' attitudes toward wild country.

Probably of even more importance to wilderness preservation was the "shock," as Frederick Jackson Turner called it, with which many Americans realized that the frontier was vanishing. Although he did not advocate wilderness preservation, Turner was among the first to formulate a fully developed theory about the importance of the frontier in American life. He argued in 1893 that American traits such as hardihood, self-reliance and a democratic outlook had developed from and been sustained by contact with frontier conditions. Turner spoke with foreboding of the effect its passing would have on American culture. These and similar ideas stimulated many citizens to regret the passing of frontier conditions and to celebrate their preservation in wilderness areas. In 1925 Aldo Leopold, an early advocate of wilderness protection in the national forests and a brilliant conservation philosopher, made a classic statement of the problem:

There is little question that many of the attributes most distinctive of America and Americans are [due to] the impress of the wilderness and the life that accompanied it. If we have such a thing as an American culture (and I think we have), its distinguishing marks are ... distinctive characteristics of successful pioneers. These, if anything, are the indigenous part of our Americanism, the qualities that set it apart as a new rather than an imitative contribution to civilization.

Is it not a bit beside the point for us to be so solicitous about preserving those institutions without giving so much as a thought to preserving the environment which produced them and which may now be one of our effective means of keeping them alive?

Leopold's argument embarrassed opponents of wilderness because to deny the value of wild country was to gainsay "sacred" American virtues. Amidst the uncertainties of global warfare and economic depression, wilderness as a "root" of American civilization assumed a new meaning and a new importance.

Another major idea in the rationale that was gradually formulated for wilderness in the 20th century stemmed from the belief that life in civilization failed to provide all the elements essential to man's physical, mental and spiritual welfare. Sigurd Olson's experience as a wilderness guide in the Quetico-Superior country on the Minnesota-Ontario border taught him the effect wilderness could have on tired, over-civilized men. There were some people, Olson wrote, who needed wilderness as a means of gaining "perspective" which came from solitude, serenity and the chance to meditate. "They go to it," he continued, "once a month or once a year as a sick man might go to his physician." A wilderness explorer and member of the United States Forest Service, Robert Marshall, agreed that wild country afforded the necessary means of temporarily abandoning a way of life that had become an "endless chain of mechanization and artificiality." And a justice of the United States Supreme Court recognized, as had Emerson a century before, that in the wilderness man "can come to know both himself and God." In the 20th century, however, more emphasis was usually placed on man's welfare than on communion with God.

Wilderness also offered man the challenge of struggle and accomplishment apart from the restraints of civilization that were often so frustrating and artificial. Some Americans began to realize with Thoreau that man paid a price for a surfeit of comfort and ease. As increasing scientific and technological achievement seemed only to make civilized life increasingly complex and confusing, periodic contact with wilderness, the fulfillment of man's chronic desire to "get away from it all," took on fresh importance. Related to this was the nostalgic remembrance on the part of many Americans of the semi-mythical yeoman farmer of their nation's past who, it was thought, lived happily and virtuously close to nature. Although wilderness was not the environment of the yeoman, wilderness preservation was a step away from commercialism and urbanism and as such appealed to many who looked wistfully back to a simple agrarian society.

Unlike most organisms, man has the power to change drastically the physical character of his environment. The extinction of the passenger pigeon, the devastation wrought by silt-laden flood waters, and the billowing clouds of dust which rose over the Middle West in the 1930's were forceful evidence that he had frequently used this power in a wasteful and destructive manner. Against the somber background of the results of man's heedless exploitation of his environment arose the argument for wilderness preserves as "islands" of healthy, unmodified land in which living things existed in a state of harmony and balance with each other. Ecologists, who study the relation of organisms to their environment, claimed that the opportunities wilderness afforded for study were invaluable. Aldo Leopold put the case for wilderness on an ethical plane, declaring that from wild country man could learn his dependency on the rest of the environment and the wisdom of replacing his arrogant attitude with one of humility and respect. Leopold felt that contact with wilderness encouraged the discard of the pioneer ethic of conquest and exploitation and the adoption of a "land ethic" which made man aware that the land and its innumerable life forms was a community to which he belonged, not a commodity which he possessed.

While the nostalgia for the vanishing frontier, the need for an antidote to civilization, and the importance of an harmonious man-land relationship were winning support for wilderness, the actual preservation of wild country continued. Other national parks with extensive wilderness areas followed Yosemite and Yellowstone: Mount Rainier in 1899, Glacier in 1910 and Rocky Mountain in 1915. Only three years after Hetch Hetchy, Congress passed the National Parks Act which ruled out economic usage of all present and future parks. In 1921 Aldo Leopold's article in the *Journal of Forestry* and his personal efforts as a member of the United States Forest Service launched a campaign for the establishment of a wilderness system in the national forests. Three years later the over a half million acres of the Datil (now Gila) National Forest in New Mexico were designated a wilderness area from which road building and lumbering were excluded. This was a radical departure from traditional Forest Service policy which had been directed toward managing the forests for economic use. Other wilderness preserves on national forest land followed the Gila, and in 1929 and 1939 Forest Service regulations clarified and confirmed the principle of keeping wild country wild. In 1960 the Multiple Use Act gave legal sanction to wilderness preservation in portions of the national forests. In addition to Federal action, several states undertook the protection of wilderness, notably Maine with the Baxter State Park and New York with its Adirondack reservation. Some wilderness in the 20th century still existed outside federally and state protected areas, but it was increasingly subjected to pressure for economic use and development.

Even in legal preserves, wilderness was far from inviolate. There was the chronic demand from local and regional interests to "open" protected areas to lumbering, grazing and mining as well as hydroelectric construction. In addition, the development of wilderness with roads and tourist concessions designed to meet mass recreational demands posed an increasingly serious threat to their wild status. Consequently, there followed after Hetch Hetchy a series of controversies over particular wilderness areas. The Wilderness Society, founded in 1935, with headquarters in Washington, D.C., joined the Sierra Club as a major defender of wild country before Congress and the American people. Time and again it came to the aid of wilderness under pressure from an expanding civilization. Minnesota's Quetico-Superior country, the Everglades in Florida, the Adirondacks and Washington's Olympic Peninsula were the subject of long and bitter controversy.

The biggest wilderness fight of all occurred in the 1950's and was remarkably similar to the Hetch Hetchy controversy of a half century before. A proposed Bureau of Reclamation dam on the Green River threatened the 320-square-mile Dinosaur National Monument that sprawled across the Colorado-Utah border. The ensuing debate reached national proportions with lead articles in periodicals such as *Life, Saturday Evening Post* and *Collier's,* and it dominated the discussion of conservation issues in Congress. In many respects the Echo Park controversy (the dam was to be built at Echo Park) was a test case and was recognized as such by friends of the wilderness as well as proponents of regional development. "Let's open [the Echo Park controversy] to its ultimate and inevitable extent," said William Voigt representing the Izaac

Walton League at a hearing in 1950 before the Secretary of the Interior,
"and let's settle . . . once and for all time . . . whether we may have . . . wilderness
areas . . . in these United States." Recognizing its wider import, defenders of
wilderness brought every weapon at their command into play. Considerable
pressure was brought to bear on Congress through an aroused public. At
Congressional hearings preservationists made a strong case for the importance
of wilderness based on the arguments put forward by thinkers from Thoreau to
Leopold. In the winter of 1955–1956 the Echo Park dam was dropped
from the Colorado River Storage Project and wilderness preservation as a
principle of land use had been vindicated.

A basic factor in the Echo Park triumph was the change in public attitude
toward wilderness over the course of American history. The defense of Dinosaur
National Monument would have been impossible a century before or even a
half century as the Hetch Hetchy verdict demonstrated. At either time the
preservation of Dinosaur would have violated deeply rooted assumptions about
the purpose of American civilization and of undeveloped country. But the
Echo Park triumph was not so much a victory of "higher values" over
utilitarianism and material progress as it was an indication that a mature
civilization coveted both.

Shortly after Echo Park, bills were introduced in Congress to establish a
national wilderness preservation system. Since its proposal the so-called
wilderness bill has been rewritten numerous times and 2,500 pages of testimony
have been collected at various hearings. If enacted, the bill would place a
statutory cloak of authority for wilderness preservation over about 150 separate
areas of federally controlled land mostly in the national parks and national
forests. About 40,000,000 acres would be included in the system and more
could be added. The bill declared that it was the intent of Congress "to secure for
the Americans of present and future generations the benefits of an enduring
resource of wilderness."

The establishment of a national system for wilderness preservation would
climax over a century of agitation for the protection of wild country. It would
also testify to the growth and refinement in American thought of the idea
that wilderness had important and irreplaceable non-economic values for
American civilization.

two fulfilling american democracy: the conservation movement

JAMES LEONARD BATES

*The disappearance of the American wilderness, and the
anticipated exhaustion of necessary natural resources,
sparked the first conservation crusade during the first two
decades of this century. The progressive conservationists
saw themselves as servants of the people, battling the
ignorance and greed that were entrenched in the private
sector of society. This interpretation has been adopted by
James Leonard Bates (b. 1919) who took his Ph.D. at
the University of North Carolina and now teaches at the
University of Illinois. He is also the author of* Origins of
Teapot Dome *(1963), a standard history of the oil
scandal that took place during the Harding administration.*

"Conservation," as related to an evolving government policy
in the twentieth century, has not been a clearly defined
term. For average citizens it has meant in a general way the
prevention of waste. For scholars and government
administrators it has frequently meant a little more
definitely the careful management of natural resources.

Source: James Leonard Bates, "Fulfilling American Democracy:
The Conservation Movement, 1907 to 1921," *Mississippi Valley
Historical Review* 44 (June 1957): 29–57. Reprinted by permission
of the publisher.

Herbert Hoover as food administrator in World War I and as secretary of commerce in the early 1920's helped to popularize such a concept, with emphasis on efficiency of use. There is much to be said for this construction. The acceptance of conservation in a broad sense represents a considerable advance from the nineteenth century when with a few notable exceptions squandering of public and private resources went on recklessly and often cynically. Moreover, its acceptance was a tribute to a group of men whose concept of official responsibility for conservation was not a loose, vague theory, nor a matter of efficiency as such, but a fighting, democratic faith.

Historians of modern reform have given scant attention to a rationale of conservation or to conservation as a democratic movement. In fact the program associated with Theodore Roosevelt and Gifford Pinchot is occasionally disparaged as largely sound and fury. Doubtless the ambiguity and complexity of "conservation" have tended to obscure its democratic implications. Then too, this policy was both a product of and a stimulant to the larger, so-called Progressive Movement; it shared in certain weaknesses of this epoch of reform and has shared in the criticism. The usual interpretation today is that the Progressive Movement was essentially an uprising of the middle class, protesting against monopoly and boss control of politics, stressing heavily the virtues of competition, freedom, and morality. With respect to conservation this view leads to the criticism that there existed a fundamental inconsistency between the ideas of protecting natural resources and the dominant beliefs in individualism and competition with the resultant low prices, heavy consumption, and waste.

There was another side to the Progressive Movement—perhaps the most significant side: the decline of laissez faire, the development of a social conscience, the repudiation of Social Darwinism. Most leaders of progressivism believed in a positive state. Some came to believe in the sort of factory and social legislation, welfare action, utility regulation, and limited government ownership that is associated with the New Deal. A few wished to go farther than the New Deal ever went. While the conservationists, like others progressively inclined, differed among themselves, nevertheless they had a program which may be described as limited socialism in the public interest. Influenced by Henry George, Edward Bellamy, Lester Ward, William James, Arthur Twining Hadley, Thorstein Veblen, Charles A. Beard, and others, these protectors of the public lands were far removed from classical economics.

The organized conservationists were concerned more with economic justice and democracy in the handling of resources than with mere prevention of waste. One aspect of the matter was the price and income situation, the actual monetary rewards from the marvelous wealth of this land. Conservationists believed that somehow the common heritage, the socially created resources and institutions, had passed into the hands of vested interests and that the benefits were siphoned into the hands of a few. There were several ways in which this situation might be remedied, as they saw it: first, to hold on to the remaining public lands, at least temporarily, preventing further monopolization; second, to attempt to give the people a fuller share of opportunities and profits; and finally, in that period of low income to keep prices proportionately low.

The monopolists who jacked up prices were anathema, even though their methods might contribute to conservation by reducing consumption. Conservation through penalizing the public was something which democratically motivated leaders were not prepared to accept.

The conservationists' approach was broad. They believed in government studies and safeguards for the preservation of irreplaceable resources such as petroleum; they recognized and struggled with problems which remain today only partially solved. They understood the need for federal leadership in an organic structure based on the unity of nature itself. As early as 1910 Gifford Pinchot proclaimed, "Every river is a unit from its source to its mouth." They made mistakes, of course. Like most progressives, they concluded easily that the opposition on a particular issue consisted of "robber barons," conspirators, and frauds. Yet at times they were capable of a surprising detachment; a key conservationist, for example, referred admiringly to a "very scholarly and fine" argument that the public domain should be turned over to the states.

In a sense the conservation movement was a nonpartisan, statesmanlike cause, winning support from scientists, politicians, and others all over the country. But a fact of long-range significance was its Republican origin; Republicans led by Pinchot and Roosevelt were the main inspiration of this program. These men were proud of their work, many of them almost fanatically devoted to Roosevelt. They did not easily dissociate the Republican party or the "Republican Roosevelt," who had first given them their chance, from the body of their accomplishments. Politics and personalities help appreciably to explain the conservation fight from 1907 to 1921.

In tracing the growth of a new attitude toward public resources it would be inaccurate to give credit only to the Republicans. This enlightenment was evolutionary, like reform in general, and Grover Cleveland, William A. J. Sparks as land commissioner, Hoke Smith as secretary of the interior, and other Democrats in later years made important contributions. Even so, the concern here is with the full-fledged movement to which was given in 1907 the name "conservation." There is no doubt that progressive Republicans were the main actors.

Albert J. Beveridge of Indiana, United States senator, 1899–1911, a Republican and a progressive, was among those who witnessed the beginnings of the conservation policy. In 1921 he wrote to Gifford Pinchot:

So, time, and time, and time again I thought of you, and the notable work you began more than twenty years ago, and have steadily pursued ever since, to save the country's woodland resources; and it suggested to me again your magnificent statesmanship known as the Conservation policy. For it is statesmanship, real statesmanship of the highest order. You may recall that after breakfast at your house, when you had developed your idea and before you presented it to President Roosevelt, you outlined it to me, and I said to you that forenoon that it was the biggest piece of constructive statesmanship that I had run across. . . . The whole Conservation system is yours, dear Gifford. I honestly think that you have done more than any other

man for the future well-being of the Republic; and I have said this
publicly as well as privately on every appropriate occasion—and I intend
to go on saying it.

Pinchot remembered "with keen interest and satisfaction" the beginnings
of this movement as described by Beveridge, and in 1937 he recalled further:
"The idea was so new that it did not even have a name. Of course it had to have
a name. Our little inside group discussed it a great deal. Finally Overton Price
suggested that we should call it 'conservation' and the President said 'O. K.'
So we called it the conservation movement."

Allowing for exaggeration on the part of Pinchot and his friends, it is
doubtless true that he and Roosevelt inspired this movement. Gifford Pinchot,
the son of a Pennsylvania landowner, businessman, philanthropist, and patron of
the arts, was stimulated to an early interest in forestry. His father, James W.
Pinchot, recommended forestry as a profession, having seen it practiced in
Europe but not in this country. The young Pinchot was captivated by the idea.
Finding no genuine forestry course in the United States after his graduation
from Yale in 1889, he went to Europe to study. On returning, he became forester
at George Vanderbilt's Biltmore Estate, near Asheville, North Carolina. In
1896 he was appointed to the National Forest Commission and assigned
the task of surveying United States forest resources. His reputation now
established, in 1898 he became "forester" of the Forest Division (later the Forest
Service) in the Agriculture Department, the position he held while in government
service. Pinchot had boundless energy and enthusiasm; "tree mad" some had
called him at Yale. Although not a systematic thinker, and sometimes
annoyingly platitudinous, he possessed unusual qualities of intellect, character,
and leadership. He was cultured and receptive to ideas. He was an aristocrat
devoting himself to public service, passionately concerned about economic
injustice—a fighter, a likable fellow, a good companion. Former Congressman
William Kent of California referred in 1923 to one of Pinchot's best qualities, his
"inherent modesty" and "desire to work in harmony with others."

Pinchot owed much to older men who pioneered in the scientific study of
resources, and whose influence was personal and forceful; notably John Wesley
Powell (1834–1902) and W J McGee (1853–1912). Powell is well
remembered as a naturalist, explorer of the Grand Canyon, director of the
United States Bureau of Ethnology, and director of the Geological Survey.
McGee, a remarkably versatile and influential man, had a fascinating career as
anthropologist, geologist, ethnologist, hydrologist, inventor, philosopher, author,
and public servant. He was in the Geological Survey while Powell was its
head, later headed the Bureau of Ethnology (1893–1903), and then went on
to hold numerous posts of importance. While director of the St. Louis Public
Museum, he was among those in 1907 who instigated a study of inland
waterways and thereby called attention to the physiology of natural resources—
water, land, plants, and their interrelationships. Roosevelt promptly appointed
him to the Inland Waterways Commission. While at Memphis, during a tour
of the Mississippi River, McGee, Pinchot, and others made up their minds
that the President ought to call a conference; in this way they could dramatize

their ideas and objectives. Thus the famous White House Conference; and, as Pinchot said, "the fight was on."

Prior to this conference Pinchot's Forest Service already had been fighting effectively for some of the principles of unified resource management: for a sustained yield in the national forest lands; for grazing within the forest areas on payment of a fee; for leasing of water power sites, rather than giving them up permanently to private control. In other ways as well the activities of the Forest Service were expanded; not the least influential was a skillful, vigorously conducted publicity campaign.

It was not accidental that many of the leaders associated with Pinchot after 1908 were lawyers. There were for instance James R. Garfield, son of the former president, and Walter L. Fisher of Chicago. Garfield served the Roosevelt administration first in the Department of Commerce and Labor and in 1907 became secretary of the interior, doing much to establish the conservation system. Fisher succeeded Richard A. Ballinger as secretary of the interior during the Taft administration and moved within the inner circle of conservationists. Other lawyers of importance were Philip P. Wells, George W. Woodruff, and Harry A. Slattery. These three in particular were experts in their understanding of knotty legal problems that arose from land withdrawals and impending legislation. Conservation was entering a phase by 1910 in which legal minds grappled over words and phrases or over decisions of almost appalling magnitude. Its opponents had been able to retain the finest advice; but with expert legal talent now arrayed in its support, no longer, as in the past, would the public wealth go by default.

Philip Wells and George Woodruff, like Pinchot, were graduated in the Yale class of 1889. Wells was a man of unusual attainments. After taking the bachelor's degree he went ahead to do graduate work at Yale in economics and history, and in 1900 he received his Ph.D. Not satisfied with this, he had begun the study of law at Yale and continued at Columbian (later George Washington) University in Washington, D.C. His career for a time was centered at Yale as instructor in and librarian of the Law School, as well as a lecturer in history. In 1906 Pinchot brought him to Washington where he served first as chief law officer with the Forest Service and later in the same capacity with the Reclamation Service. Both in and out of government he acted as a special adviser to Pinchot. Woodruff was a former Yale football great and a genial and able friend whom Pinchot brought into the Forest Service as his first law officer. He was soon called, however, on a special assignment to the Interior Department as an assistant attorney general. For a few months in 1907 he functioned as acting secretary of the interior. Slattery came later into the Pinchot circle. Good friends and brilliant lawyers, these men worked effectively for the principles of the conservation program.

After 1909 the rallying point for conservationists became the National Conservation Association, with headquarters in Washington, D.C. This organization grew out of the struggle between the President and Congress over executive authority in appointing commissions. Specifically, a Commission on National Conservation appointed by Roosevelt as a result of the White House Conference undertook an inventory of all resources. Its work was comprehensive

and its findings significant; but the Sixtieth Congress consented to publish
only a few copies of the report and declared that such executive commissions
were unconstitutional. Roosevelt denounced this view, and when President Taft,
as his successor, decided in 1909 that Congress perhaps was right and that the
Commission should do its work indirectly the forces of Pinchot and Roosevelt
decided that action was demanded. They formed the National Conservation
Association, a private body, with Charles W. Eliot, former president of Harvard,
serving briefly as president before being succeeded by Pinchot, with Harry
Slattery as secretary, and with Philip Wells as one of its counsel. Typical
directors in the period 1916–1917 were Jane Addams, Carrie Chapman Catt,
Samuel Gompers, Judge Ben Lindsey of Denver, and Irvine L. Lenroot
of the House of Representatives.

The National Conservation Association's effectiveness stemmed in large part
from the great abilities of Harry Slattery as executive secretary, with headquarters
near the Capitol. According to Roosevelt, the Association had first to prevent
bad legislation in order to protect public resources from monopoly control,
and second to guide through Congress the best of conservation measures.
According to McGee, it had become the "legitimate repository and exponent of
conservation doctrine, and the accepted leader of the Conservation Movement,
more especially in its moral aspect," and Charles R. Van Hise saw it as the
propaganda agent of the movement. With understandable prejudice, Pinchot
reviewed its work in 1921 and concluded that "no other Association has exerted
anything like so large an influence in proportion to its membership and
expenditures. It has overcome, not once, but many times, the efforts of the
greatest lobbies ever assembled in Washington." Each of these evaluations was
essentially true. Slattery in some respects was better qualified than Pinchot to
fight the lobbies, to make the rounds of Congress, to grind out publicity
and propaganda, and when necessary to work night and day poring over
legislation looking for ambiguities and loopholes, drawing up legislation as
he and Wells, or Lenroot, or Senator Robert M. La Follette, or others thought
it ought to be.

A native of South Carolina, Slattery completed his education at Georgetown
University and George Washington University and remained in the Washington
area. In 1909, still in his early twenties, he became secretary to Pinchot.
A short time later he took over the job with the National Conservation
Association. Slattery was an informal, amiable sort of person, folksy in his
speech but sharp of mind. People liked him and relied upon him. He was
informed on history, law, and economics, but most especially on politics and
personalities—the Washington scene. Liberal if not radical, he conceived of
himself and the Association as the "watchdog" of conservation. When Slattery
resigned as secretary in 1921 (to remain with the Association as counsel)
Pinchot remarked on his "intimate knowledge" of and close contact with
Congress. In this, he thought, Slattery stood "alone among the secretaries of
associations with headquarters in Washington." And the result had been Slattery's
"controlling part" in writing conservation principles of "immense value" into
the laws of the land. It was a generous tribute to the kind of man who so often
serves the public, with little publicity and no public recognition.

The developing rationale of the conservationists is of the utmost importance in explaining their conduct and influence. By no means were they all alike, but people such as Roosevelt, Pinchot, and La Follette believed that a larger amount of governmental interference and regulation in the public interest was required. They were especially concerned about the remaining public lands, which, according to principles grounded in the Homestead and other acts, belonged to all. Millions of acres had been given away or sold to corporate interests for a trifling price or had been actually stolen. This record of carelessness and exploitation could not be expunged. However, to conserve and use wisely that which remained, to show that civilized man could profit from mistakes of the past, to democratize the handling of a common heritage, would be a genuine consolation. A crisis, they felt, existed. Such an attitude was a compound of idealism, passion, and sober analysis. These men realized that American society in the twentieth century must be increasingly one of co-operative and collective gains.

As progressives they agreed passionately on the need for honesty and a social conscience in the administration of resources. Declared Pinchot in 1910: "There is no hunger like land hunger, and no object for which men are more ready to use unfair and desperate means than the acquisition of land." Americans had to make up their minds whether their political system was to be devoted to "unclean money or free men." It was fortunate, he believed, that special interests were afflicted with a "blindness" because of their "wholly commercialized point of view." Conservationists were convinced that hostility toward materialism and toward money men and special interests usually was warranted, that history afforded ample justification for suspicion. If nothing else united the conservationists, there was this hatred of the boodler, the rank materialist, the exploiter.

Intellectually there was much that drew these men together. McGee, whom Pinchot called "the scientific brains" of the conservation movement, provided a rationale for action. "Every revolution," said McGee, "whatever its material manifestations . . . is first and foremost a revolution in thought and spirit." Believing that Americans had largely lost their rights in the land, McGee felt that knowledge of how this had occurred might yet insure the "perpetuity" of the people.

From the early beginnings of the United States there had been confusion and carelessness in the administration of "land," a word identified with resources generally: "When Independence was declared and the Constitution was framed, no resources were reckoned except the Men who made the nation and the Land on which they lived." Trees were considered an obstacle to be burned or girdled; little attention was paid to natural growth above or minerals below. The "Fathers," filled with their dreams of a freehold citizenry rooted in the soil, proceeded to dissipate values other than the land itself. The results were both good and evil. So far as certain farsighted or favored individuals were concerned, the way was opened to wealth, power, and monopoly. McGee wrote: "the resources passed under monopolistic control with a rapidity never before seen in all the world's history; and it is hardly too much to say that the Nation has become one of the Captains of Industry first, and one of the

People and their chosen representatives only second." Moreover, the "free gift" of resources "under the title of land" defeated the original purpose of creating a free independent citizenry. The people had become "industrial dependents." Incidental to this process of resource appropriation was waste.

"Ample resources" remained, it was true, but what was to be done with them? Should the "People," whose work and travail had created this wealth, receive the benefits? Or should they go "into the hands of the self-chosen and self-annointed [sic] few, largely to forge new shackles for the wrists and ankles of the many?" Deliberately and thoughtfully, McGee argued, American freemen must proceed "to reclaim their own." Theodore Roosevelt's opening address at the White House Conference expounded on the same theme—the right of the people to public wealth and, moreover, their right to control *private* property for the common weal. He quoted the high authority of Justice Holmes, speaking for the Supreme Court with respect to state protection of water, forests, and the atmosphere: "This public interest is omnipresent wherever there is a State, and grows more pressing as population grows." And Roosevelt added emphatically that the dictum was to be carried farther than the forests and the streams.

McGee's indebtedness to Henry George is obvious. As a product of the exciting generation in which Social Darwinism was elaborated and then repudiated, as an associate of such men as John Wesley Powell and Lester Ward, it was not strange that McGee emphasized economic justice. The Bill of Rights must be purified, he said, through equal opportunities and equal rights in the common resources. He stressed the "trinity" of liberty, equality, and fraternity. The keynote was fraternity. There remained to be established "full brotherhood among men and generations." Pinchot, advancing similar arguments, thought that the answer lay in the conservation movement, the most democratic that the country had known in a generation.

Philip Wells became more explicit about the ideas and hopes which had driven him and his associates "in the conservation fight." They had been concerned with economic justice and incidentally with waste because if the resources were destroyed nothing remained upon which the principle of justice could operate. In the light of the American system, he said, they conceived of economic justice as meaning that "so far as possible within the general limitations fixed by popular opinion as to fundamentals, and within the specific limitations fixed by constitutional provisions, the 'economic rent,' present and future ('unearned increment') in natural resources should be retained by the public which should also see that the resources are not wasted in order that the benefits of the new policy may be prolonged as far into the future as possible." While at Yale, Wells had studied under William Graham Sumner, who once remarked that every man was either a socialist or an anarchist. Actually, Wells believed, most people were somewhere between these two poles. "Now the conservationists as to specific natural resources (water power, forests, the mineral fuels and mineral fertilizers) inclined to the socializing pole; that is, they sought to enlarge the public control of these resources . . . both for the prevention of waste and, more essential, for the socializing of the raw resource value including unearned increment."

Wells went ahead to discuss Henry George, "a constructive economist of very high order" rather than a crank, as some maintained, and to compare his philosophy with that of the conservationists. They differed in that George was essentially an individualist, of the "Neo-Manchester School." They had agreed in "trying to socialize raw resource value," George attempting to do this through his single tax on unearned increments and with slight regard for constitutional problems. The conservationists, on the other hand, were interested primarily in "selected resources exhaustible or subject to great waste, suitable for development only or chiefly by large aggregations of capital and peculiarly open to monopolistic abuse." They differed further as to ideas of management, Wells continued. "The conservationists want to socialize to a certain extent the management of their selected resources (as the Forest Service does in selling standing timber in a National Forest by restrictions imposed on logging methods to secure a new timber crop); whereas George would anarchize the management of all natural resources by turning them over to unrestricted private ownership."

Pinchot and his group therefore believed in using the authority of federal and state government to compel conservation practices ("socialization of management"), even aiming to do this on *private* forest lands. With respect to the alternatives of federal or state action Pinchot once remarked: "I have very little interest in the abstract question whether the nation is encroaching upon the rights of the states or the states upon the nation. Power falls naturally to that person or agency which can and does use it, and . . . the nation acts . . . [while] the states do not."

The influence of these ideas and the impact of the Pinchot organization cannot be minimized. Nevertheless, Pinchot and his friends did not constitute the entire conservation movement. There were issues which inevitably divided the conservationists as a whole: the clashing of personalities and ambitions, disagreement over methods if not over goals, disputes between Democrats and Republicans, and economic sectionalism especially as it arose between the West and the East. Any issue or event could impinge upon conservation with divisive results or with diverse and complicating effects—for example World War I. In general, one accepting the designation of "conservationist" was a progressive, believing in the necessity of strong executive leadership and federal action. He might be a radical or an outright socialist. Frequently, on the other hand, he emphasized as heavily as did President Taft the authority of Congress, the statutory system that must be erected, the quieting of any doubts as to constitutionality. And it was not strange for a conservationist to consider himself a conservative; one who believed in honest government and orderly processes, who hated boodling, who watched vigilantly for the sly steals that special interests might perpetrate. Representative James R. Mann of Illinois, for example, might be linked politically with "Uncle Joe" Cannon's Old Guard, but the Pinchot forces treasured him as one of their most dependable allies. Regionally speaking, the southerner who favored conservation differed from the northerner or from the westerner. Southerners were much influenced by traditions of agrarianism and anti-monopoly action as well as by the fact

and who now in the same selfish way was doing all he could to block Lenroot's ambitions.

At the same time, however, the forces of La Follette and Pinchot could work together in February–March, 1919, to defeat the so-called Pittman mineral leasing bill, an anti-conservationist measure which they considered peculiarly obnoxious. On matters of principle, they could unite; but Slattery, Wells, and company of the National Conservation Association took pains not to "get the wires crossed" between La Follette and Lenroot when needing so keenly the help of both. It was La Follette finally, not Lenroot, who saved them in the petroleum fight, La Follette who argued and filibustered successfully against the mineral leasing bill with materials supplied by the Association. And two years later it was La Follette, again assisted by Slattery and Wells, who instigated the Teapot Dome investigation.

La Follette and Pinchot operated differently, and this was no discredit to either. The Wisconsinite had neither the disposition nor the opportunity for bartering favors with Wilson (after 1916), nor with Harding, Coolidge, and others of the Republican Old Guard. His forte was to attack, to filibuster, to block "giveaways," to tack on remedial amendments, to force concessions, to rally the left wing. With Pinchot it was a different story. In each Congress, in each administration, Pinchot as president of the National Conservation Association would try to place his men, would distribute his propaganda, would try to win support. Just as the special interests lobbied to control or influence policy, so would he. As an additional moderating influence there were without doubt Pinchot's political ambitions. He was available, for instance, for a place in Harding's cabinet, and a conciliatory course was sometimes prudent. He would agitate from within if possible, or he would attack from without if necessary.

In their proposals for control of public lands, the two men differed only slightly. In La Follette's opinion there had been only one great issue in all of history: a struggle "between labor and those who would control, through slavery in one form or another, the laborers." Uppermost in his consideration, therefore, was justice for the exploited. With respect to public resources in general, he argued that there must be a policy of continuing public ownership, of leasing where possible, of price controls, and a degree of government operation depending upon the monopoly situation. Basic raw materials, even though privately owned, must sell at a reasonable price and if they did not he advocated government appropriation. Quite early he had called for leasing rather than selling government properties, and in the conservation fight of the late Wilson years he stressed a leasing system for coal and oil and other nonmetalliferous minerals but not without adequate safeguards for democratic development and prevention of waste. He believed, for example, that evidence of collusive bargaining and fixing of prices among the lessees should warrant government cancellation of the lease. There were some who charged that La Follette hoped actually to destroy the leasing bills and in time to substitute his own "socialistic" schemes.

The coming of a Democratic administration in 1913 produced a reorientation affecting everyone in the fight for conservation. This was due partly to the status of the withdrawal question; nonmetallic mineral lands and water power sites no longer were being sold or given away and had to be made available under some scheme for development. Prior to 1913, Republicans had argued mostly among themselves; they could now sit back and watch the Democrats undertake the direction of policy, and could wait for an appropriate occasion to assail and expose them. Wilson believed in conservation, and the policy of his administration was directed toward formulation of a leasing system. But on the question of how this should be done his own advisers were often in sharp disagreement, thereby giving the Republicans their opportunity for criticism. In the beginning, La Follette, Pinchot, and many Republicans of a progressive mind were sympathetic to Wilson's program. A few turned against him by 1916; many others by 1918; and by 1920 their abandonment was almost complete.

World War I and industrial mobilization were largely responsible for this time of trouble. Of deepest concern to the organized conservationists was this question: How disinterested, how patriotic, were the businessmen who came streaming into Wilson's government for the purpose of preparing the nation for war? In the attitude of conservationists toward dollar-a-year men one finds new evidence that their aims went far beyond the mere prevention of waste. They were concerned with problems of men against money, with profiteering, with economic justice, with maintaining democracy. By these standards Wilson qualified, at the least, as a moderate conservationist. He believed that leasing laws opening western lands to development must be passed; that the war (creating new demands for petroleum and other resources) made a solution most urgent; and that a compromise doing justice to all parties could be effected. Wilson was cautious and showed a wariness about the possibility of profiteering and corruption under cloak of war.

Wilson's secretary of the navy, Josephus Daniels, going beyond wariness, was absolutely convinced that the special interests were using the war emergency for purposes of grabbing resources belonging to all the people. La Follette, Pinchot, and most of the progressive Republicans agreed. Slattery, writing from Washington, expressed the attitude of the National Conservation Association when he referred to that "National Council of Defense outfit." "We have been surrounded with them . . . and I have from the start had my strong suspicions about the whole bunch." Slattery and Gifford Pinchot feared that Secretary of the Interior Franklin K. Lane was "going to give away every thing in sight" before the war had ended, unless they stopped him. Slattery picturesquely summed up the whole situation: It looked as though "these bushwhacking gentlemen," while good people had their faces turned to the war, were going to "raid the 'smokehouse and hen-roost' as of border-war days." Slattery and his associates had in mind particular bushwhackers, such as John D. Ryan and C. F. Kelley of the Anaconda Copper Company and Edward L. Doheny of the Pan-American Petroleum Company.

One effect of the southern leadership in the Wilson administration was to stimulate sectional rivalries, with some important effects upon conservation. The western states resisted at first a federal program for the public lands while eastern and southern leaders were forcing the issue. But the native South of

Woodrow Wilson differed somewhat from the East of Gifford Pinchot.
In brief, the East-West division over conservation was accompanied in the
Wilson years by a flare-up of North-South animosities. There had been nothing
like it since the 1890's, perhaps since Reconstruction. Some applied the term
of Reconstruction days, "waving the bloody shirt," to the divisive strategy
of Republican politicians, who urged their constituents to vote for Republicans
since only in that way could the power of southern Democrats be broken.
To measure the importance of these sectional feelings is difficult, but that they
existed and exerted an influence of subtle though powerful proportions is
certain.

The organized conservationists from the start had resisted as best they could
the regional prejudices that might reduce their influence on policy or disrupt
their plans in Congress. Nevertheless, as advocates of a withdrawal policy
they had to face intrenched hostility from many western interests. The
conservationists were of course convinced that their policies benefited the
western people, as distinguished from the big interests. They were correct in
asserting, as Pinchot did, that "monopolistic control was infinitely more potent
in the West . . . than in the East." It was in this region of the enterprising
pioneer and the free individual that the special interests attained their most
ruthless power. The Southern Pacific Railroad, the Standard Oil Company
of California, Colorado's corporate interests or "the Beast" (as described by
Judge Ben Lindsey), the Phelps Dodge corporation in Arizona, and the Anaconda
Copper Company of Montana (Standard Oil) were notorious examples.
Edward L. Doheny's Pan-American Petroleum Company and Harry Sinclair's
Mammoth Oil Company were worthy inheritors of at least a portion of this
tradition—that the United States government was fair game.

The West, however, was always divided. Men like Representative William
Kent and Governor George C. Pardee of California, Judge Ben Lindsey of
Colorado, Senator John B. Kendrick of Wyoming, and Governor Joseph M.
Dixon of Montana were in the conservationist camp. The trend in the Progressive
Era was conservationist. Roosevelt's dramatic flair was combined with Pinchot's
incessant labors for the cause. It was formidable propaganda for the justice,
wisdom, and democracy of the federal government's program. Western
senators and representatives, who had been almost unanimous against the land
withdrawals, who favored the old policy of gift and sale, slowly had to
recognize the handwriting on the wall. Public sentiment had come to favor
the forest reserves, the government retention of mineral areas and water power
sites, and an active federal policy. As Senator Walsh of Montana saw the
situation in 1919, it was "useless" to declaim against leasing. "Almost every
western Senator has protested loud and long and often. It is a condition
and not a theory that confronts us." If these lands were to be developed, he
concluded, Congressmen had better compromise on a leasing bill. One incentive
to compromise was the probability that western states would share handsomely
in royalties accruing from federal lands within their borders. To some,
compromise seemed in the air; sectionalism seemed on the decline.

Though the West and the South have often been allied in politics, they seldom
were allied on conservation policy. Slattery suggested that the South's residue

of state-rights feeling accounted for its apparent lack of interest in the support of federal measures to regulate resources, but as a matter of fact the anti-conservationists got little comfort from below the Mason and Dixon line. Edward T. Taylor, a Democratic representative from Colorado and one of the die-hards opposing conservation, took note of this fact in 1914. Referring to the southern failure to help the West by resisting "carpetbag control" from Washington, Taylor said: "I want to say to my genial friends from the sunny South that during my six years of service in this House I never yet have been able to understand why the members from the Southern states, that had such a long and serious experience in being governed by appointive officials from Washington, controlled by nonresident officers, can not only complacently vote for but work for propositions controlling our western states . . . from Washington."

Among the Democrats who contributed importantly to the promotion of the Roosevelt-Pinchot program or its continuation under Wilson were such southerners or border-state men as Representatives William B. Craig (Alabama), Scott Ferris (Oklahoma), and Asbury F. Lever (South Carolina), Attorneys General James C. McReynolds (Tennessee) and Thomas W. Gregory (Texas), Secretary of the Navy Josephus Daniels (North Carolina), and Senator Claude A. Swanson (Virginia). Some co-operated with the National Conservation Association, dominated by Pinchot; and Ferris, chairman of the House Committee on Public Lands from 1913 to 1919, enjoyed the confidence of both President Wilson and the Association. In 1918, however, Slattery wrote: "Ferris has recently been made Chairman of the Democratic Congressional Committee, which is certainly an unfortunate thing for us. Politics will begin undoubtedly to have quite a sweep with him, and we will certainly have to watch him from now on." Secretary Daniels and Attorney General Gregory enjoyed good relations with the Pinchot group as well as with La Follette. Their principles were much the same, and all contributed toward forcing a compromise on leasing, in which the special claimants to public lands, some of them fraudulent, would be granted a minimum of their demands.

The Northeast and the Southeast, in effect, were able at last to force a leasing system upon the West. The passage of the Water Power Act and the Mineral Leasing Act of 1920 inaugurated a new policy of continuing public ownership and federal trusteeship in which conservation and the national interest seemed to be the winners. These laws, said Senator Walsh, would be regarded in the future as a landmark no less important to western people than the Homestead Act of 1862 or the Mining Act of 1872. Pinchot declared that the major portion of the Roosevelt program had now been achieved. Slattery, Wells, La Follette, and Daniels were among those who in spite of a few doubts indicated general satisfaction with the compromise. Undoubtedly they had won something of a victory and the way had been prepared for a larger federal role in the future. The leasing laws of 1920 grew, however, from a long struggle, involving many people who remembered clearly the controversies of the recent past. To separate this and other conservation issues from the pall of suspicions and hatreds in 1918–1921 is impossible.

There was a special rancor after the passage of the leasing acts. Democrats claimed this legislation as an achievement for their party. The Republican conservationists retorted that they had originated this program; that without the vigilance of Pinchot and La Follette bad bills would have passed; and that the Sixty-sixth Congress, in which the compromise had been attained, was a Republican Congress elected in 1918.

Progressive Republicans of the Pinchot variety developed a distrust for "southern reactionaries" and others in the Wilson administration. They regarded as exceptions such men as Josephus Daniels or Thomas W. Gregory. Even President Wilson, they believed, had betrayed them at a critical point in the leasing fight by giving his support to the notorious Pittman bill in February, 1919. Those for whom conservationists reserved a special contempt were Secretary Lane, A. Mitchell Palmer (who succeeded Gregory as attorney general in 1919), and Albert S. Burleson, the postmaster general. Certain Democratic senators were almost in the same class—the "western crowd" including Key Pittman of Nevada, James D. Phelan of California, Charles S. Thomas of Colorado, and Walsh of Montana (coupled with Republicans like Reed Smoot of Utah and Albert B. Fall of New Mexico).

Lane and Palmer were favorite targets, regarded as being worse than Richard Ballinger. Lane's administration was, and will continue to be, controversial; for he was a complex personality, and his seven years in office were critical for the conservation movement and for the security of the nation itself. Conservationists were convinced quite early in the Wilson years that Lane had turned out to be a dissembler, coming to Washington as a progressive from California, talking the language of an idealist and a conservationist, but siding in fact with special business interests. It is clear, however, that Lane did change after 1913, becoming pro-business in outlook, and though he often played the role of conservationist his heart lay with "the American Pioneer." Palmer became persona non grata to progressives of both parties because of his role in the "Red Scare"; but more than that, as attorney general he assumed authority over the disposition of many public land cases, including petroleum cases in California, and was regarded as having failed to protect the public interest. The progressive Republicans who had initiated conservation came to feel, therefore, that the Wilson administration had badly deteriorated and was no longer to be trusted. They hoped that their own party, after winning the election of 1920, would do better.

Conservation had arrived at a crisis in 1920–1921 more serious than its adherents suspected. Their achievements were not quite so momentous nor so unshakeable as they liked to believe. Political partisanship had become intensified; co-operation between northerners and southerners in behalf of conservation had been rendered more difficult. Albert B. Fall and others who shared his views were moving into positions of responsibility. Many honest men during the 1920's declared for a watered-down version of conservation almost synonymous with business efficiency or gave serious consideration to plans for turning public lands over to the states. Business organizations appropriated, with more or less sincerity, the word "conservation." If ever an opportunity afforded itself for the rejection of Pinchot's ideals concerning democracy in resource use, this was the time.

Conservation not only survived the 1920's; it emerged in some respects stronger than ever. William Kent had observed in 1919 that the conservation principles were gaining acceptance all over the West and that, moreover, many of the ideals growing out of this movement were affecting sentiment in all directions. His own work in conservation had been of all his efforts the most satisfying and constructive. In 1923 Governor Joseph M. Dixon of Montana, the old "Bull Mooser" then engaged in a bitter struggle against the Anaconda Copper Company, remarked on the growing popularity of the conservation policy. Even its enemies in the West were being converted, he wrote to Pinchot. "It would surprise you to know with what unanimity the people of the West now acquiesce to your own far-sighted vision of thirty years ago. The old crowd that fought so viciously against any governmental regulations of the forest and range are now your most pronounced friends. On several occasions during public talks, I have taken some satisfaction in 'rubbing it in' by telling them that 'Gifford Pinchot saved us [Westerners] from ourselves'." At the height of the Teapot Dome scandal in 1924 Pinchot declared: "So far the only clear thing about it all seems to be that the conservation policy has once more completely defeated its enemies, and is more strongly intrenched in the public confidence and consideration than ever before."

In spite of its complexity, in spite of its ambiguity, the conservation policy contained an inner vitality that could not be obscured or destroyed. Here was an effort to implement democracy for twentieth-century America, to stop the stealing and exploitation, to inspire high standards of government, to preserve the beauty of mountain and stream, to distribute more equitably the profits of this economy. From McGee, to Pinchot and La Follette, to George Norris and Harold Ickes, to Wayne Morse and Lister Hill—there has burned a democratic zeal, a social faith. The faith was genuine; the propaganda effective. Though a careful evaluation of the impact upon this country remains to be made, it is difficult to escape the conclusion that a fighting band of conservationists has made the United States much richer in material wealth and in the democratic spirit and faith of its people.

three
the conservation movement and the progressive tradition

SAMUEL P. HAYS

The principal alternative to Bates's view of conservation as
triumphant democracy was proposed by Samuel P. Hays
(b. 1921) in Conservation and the Gospel of Efficiency
(1959). His argument dovetails nicely with the growing
revision of the whole Progressive Era, a revision placing
more emphasis on the role of businessmen and technicians
in forming—*rather than merely resisting—the political*
concerns and responses of the period. Professor Hays
is also the author of The Response to Industrialism
(1957) and has been at the University of Pittsburgh
since 1960.

The progressive revolt of the early twentieth century, so
most historians have argued, was an attempt to control
private, corporate wealth for public ends. The conservation
movement typified this spirit. According to one such writer,

. . . the progressive movement in the Republican party
during Mr. Roosevelt's administration manifested itself
primarily in a struggle against corporations. The struggle
had two phases; first and most important, was the attempt to

Samuel P. Hays, *Conservation and the Gospel of Efficiency: The*
Progressive Conservation Movement, 1890–1920 (Cambridge,
Mass.: Harvard University Press, 1959), pp. 261–76.
Copyright © 1959, by the President and Fellows of Harvard
College. Reprinted by permission of the author and the publisher.

*find some adequate means of controlling and regulating corporate
activities; and second, and almost as important, was the resistance to the
efforts of corporations to exploit the natural resources of the nation
in their own behalf.*

Professor Roy Robbins, author of the most important one-volume history of the
public lands, supports this view. He describes conservation as a popular reaction
to the post-Civil War influence of private corporations in federal public land
policy. Gifford Pinchot's autobiography, moreover, contains strong antimonopoly
overtones. He wrote: "Its [monopoly's] abolition or regulation is an inseparable
part of the conservation policy." This view has taken such deep root in the mind
of the general public that conservation crusaders need only to expose the hand of
corporate business to brand a resource measure as "anti-conservation" and
detrimental to the public interest.

OWNERSHIP OR USE?

This point of view correctly describes the ideology of the conservation movement,
but fails to analyze its broader meaning. It stresses conservation as a theory of
resource ownership when, in fact, the movement was most concerned with
resource use. To most historians the amount of exploitation in the nineteenth
century varied directly with ownership. Large corporations, they argue, wasted
resources lavishly, while small farmers did not. Professor Robbins writes: "The
agency most responsible for this exploitation was not the individual farmer who
typified the earlier period of American history, but the corporation which with
abundant capital at its disposal was able to appropriate large areas of valuable land
and often to exact an exorbitant tribute from the people who were attempting to
build up the civilization of the country." While utilizing antimonopoly overtones
to make the reasoning seem plausible, this argument actually proceeds from
premises as to land ownership to conclusions concerning land use. To support
his contention Robbins cites evidence that corporations obtained large areas of
land from the federal government and widely used fraudulent land entries to
enlarge their holdings. These facts help to establish the pattern of land ownership,
but they do not pertain to problems of land use. As Thomas C. Chamberlin,
professor of geology at the University of Chicago, wrote in 1910:

*In their fundamental nature, the problems of conservation and the
problems of possession are distinct questions, each to be solved in its
own way and on its own basis. . . . The conservation of natural
resources centers in the scientific and technical; the right of
ownership and the most desirable form of ownership center in the
political and sociological. . . . [The] ownership or distribution of
values . . . has no logical relation to conservation and may even be
incompatible with its highest realization.*

And Philip P. Wells, former law officer of the United States Forest Service,
complained in 1919 that too many writers described the conservation movement
primarily as a protest against "land grabbing."

Resource exploitation, in fact, reflected the attitude not merely of corporations, but of Americans in all walks of life. Small farmers, as well as corporate leaders, helped to establish a wasteful pattern of land use. Everyone in the nineteenth century hoped to make a killing from rising land values and from quickly extracting the cheap, virgin resources of the nation. Corporations often did exploit resources, such as the timber of the Great Lakes forest region. Such examples, however, do not support the general view that corporations by their very nature promoted resource waste, and the larger the corporation and the greater its self-interest, the more destruction it caused. On the contrary, when the conservation movement arose in the early twentieth century, it became clear that larger corporations could more readily afford to undertake conservation practices, that they alone could provide the efficiency, stability of operations, and long-range planning inherent in the conservation idea. Larger owners could best afford to undertake sustained-yield forest and range management, and understood more clearly than did small farmers the requirements for large-scale irrigation and water power development.

That large owners frequently supported conservation policies and small owners just as frequently opposed them also forces the historian to rethink the movement's significance. Many have argued that the Forest Reserve Act of 1891 and subsequent conservation measures reflected the antimonopoly movement of the post-Civil War Era. In explaining the "rise of conservation," Robbins writes:

Conviction that the federal government had been all too generous in its disposition of favors during the period between 1850 and 1870 produced a reaction in the form of an antimonopoly movement which demanded legislation to restore the public domain, and to provide equal opportunity for the many and special privilege to none. . . . Not until after the railroad magnate, the cattle king, the mining baron and the lumber monarch had established a prestige as great as that enjoyed by any capitalist of the eastern industrial order, did the federal government finally pass the first of a series of laws which was ultimately to be distinguished as the conservation movement.

Yet, antimonopolists did not conspicuously push conservation measures, and in fact frequently opposed them. The campaign to establish forest reserves had its origin not in antimonopolism, but in the drive by wilderness groups to perpetuate untouched large areas of natural beauty, by Eastern arboriculturists and botanists to save trees for the future and by Western water users, both large corporations and small owners, to preserve their water supply by controlling silting. Large cattlemen backed the range leasing measure, while settlers opposed it. Groups representing small farmers supported Pinchot during his fight for federal water power regulation, but this support came from those whose lands were threatened with flooding by proposed private water power reservoirs, and who in later years repeatedly opposed federal reservoir construction for the same reason.

The movements for wider land distribution and more efficient land use had entirely separate origins. The first continued after the Forest Reserve Act of 1891, but in a direction diametrically opposed to the spirit of that law. Homesteaders bitterly resented permanent reservation of public land from private entry. To them, forest, range, or mineral reserves differed little from withdrawals for railroad land grants. They fought with equal vigor to abolish both. At the same time, conservation leaders felt closer to the spirit of development, typified by the railroad land grants, than to the reaction against the roads. Both railroads and conservationists promoted large-scale economic development. While the conservation movement emphasized greater efficiency in this process, its goal of planned economic growth and its consolidating tendencies closely approximated the spirit of railroad construction. The transcontinental lines, in fact, cooperated closely with conservationists in developing Western resources, and gave special aid to federal irrigation, forest, and range programs.

In placing the conservation movement in the context of progressive ideology, historians have concentrated on incidents which easily fit that viewpoint and have avoided problems which it could not easily explain. They have analyzed extensively such events as the Pinchot-Ballinger controversy, Teapot Dome, the fight for water power regulation, and the growth of federal forest and oil policy. These incidents they have interpreted as struggles between private and public ownership. They have associated private ownership with the "corporation" and resource exploitation, and public ownership with the "people" and wise resource use. Historians, however, have undertaken no corresponding investigations of federal irrigation or river development. Federal range control, a crucial issue which displayed an alignment of forces exactly opposite of those indicated by the progressive ideology, received little attention until 1951. These problems played as vital a role in the Theodore Roosevelt conservation movement as did forest, mineral, and power policies. Traditional views of conservation which do not account for these developments must give way to newer interpretations.

The broader significance of the conservation movement stemmed from the role it played in the transformation of a decentralized, nontechnical, loosely organized society, where waste and inefficiency ran rampant, into a highly organized, technical, and centrally planned and directed social organization which could meet a complex world with efficiency and purpose. This spirit of efficiency appeared in many realms of American life, in the professional engineering societies, among forward-looking industrial management leaders, and in municipal government reform, as well as in the resource management concepts of Theodore Roosevelt. The possibilities of applying scientific and technical principles to resource development fired federal officials with enthusiasm for the future and imbued all in the conservation movement with a kindred spirit. These goals required public management, of the nation's streams because private enterprise could not afford to undertake it, of the Western lands to adjust one resource use to another. They also required new administrative methods, utilizing to the fullest extent the latest scientific knowledge and expert, disinterested personnel. This was the gospel of efficiency—efficiency which could be realized only through planning, foresight, and conscious purpose.

The lack of direction in American development appalled Roosevelt and his advisers. They rebelled against a belief in the automatic beneficence of unrestricted economic competition, which, they believed, created only waste, exploitation, and unproductive economic rivalry. To replace competition with economic planning, these new efficiency experts argued, would not only arrest the damage of the past, but could also create new heights of prosperity and material abundance for the future. The conservation movement did not involve a reaction against large-scale corporate business, but, in fact, shared its views in a mutual revulsion against unrestrained competition and undirected economic development. Both groups placed a premium on large-scale capital organization, technology, and industry-wide cooperation and planning to abolish the uncertainties and waste of competitive resource use.

THEODORE ROOSEVELT AND THE
CONSERVATION MOVEMENT

Historians of the Progressive Era have found it increasingly difficult to categorize Theodore Roosevelt. Was he a "liberal" or an "enlightened conservative"? Did he rob the Democrats of their reform proposals and fulfill the aims of late nineteenth-century social revolt, or did he merely mouth their causes and, in practice, betray them? These questions pose difficulties chiefly because they raise the wrong issues. They assume that the significance of Roosevelt's career lies primarily in its role in the social struggle of the late nineteenth and early twentieth centuries between the business community on the one hand and labor and farm groups on the other. On the contrary, Roosevelt was conspicuously aloof from that social struggle. He refused to become identified with it on either side. He was, in fact, predisposed to reject social conflict, in theory and practice, as the greatest danger in American society. His administration and his social and political views are significant primarily for their attempt to supplant this conflict with a "scientific" approach to social and economic questions.

Roosevelt was profoundly impressed by late nineteenth-century social unrest, and in particular by its more violent manifestations such as the Haymarket riot, the Pullman strike, Coxey's army, and the election of 1896. He viewed Populism as a class struggle which would destroy the nation through internal conflict. He rejected Western Insurgency—a continuation of Populist radicalism, he believed—because it expressed the aims of only one economic group in society which, if dominant, would exercise power as selfishly as did the Eastern business community. The economic struggle slowly evolving from rapid industrial growth aroused Roosevelt's deepest fears. His practical solution to that problem consisted neither of granting dominance to any one group, nor of creating a balance of power among all. In fact, as a result of his fear of conflict he almost denied its reality and tried to evolve concepts and techniques which would, in effect, legislate that conflict out of existence.

Social and economic problems, Roosevelt believed, should be solved, not through power politics, but by experts who would undertake scientific investigations and devise workable solutions. He had an almost unlimited faith in applied science. During his presidency, he repeatedly sought the advice of expert commissions, especially in the field of resource policy, and he looked upon the conservation movement as an attempt to apply this knowledge. But he felt that government could tackle nonresource questions such as labor problems with the same approach. In the fall of 1908 he wrote to a union official:

Already our Bureau of Labor, for the past twenty years of necessity largely a statistical bureau, is practically a Department of Sociology, aiming not only to secure exact information about industrial conditions but to discover remedies for industrial evils. . . . It is our confident claim . . . that applied science, if carried out according to our program, will succeed in achieving for humanity, above all for the city industrial worker, results even surpassing in value those today in effect on the farm.

Having little appreciation of labor's permanence as a power group in society, Roosevelt believed simply that one could approach the labor problem by improving working conditions, training more efficient employees, and stimulating the industrial machine to prevent unemployment.

President Roosevelt's abiding fear of class struggle led him to conceive of the good society as a classless society, composed, not of organized social groups, but of individuals bound together by personal relationships. Believing that "the line of division in the deeper matters of our citizenship" should "be drawn on the line of conduct," he viewed the fundamentals of social organization as personal moral qualities of honesty, integrity, frugality, loyalty, and "plain dealing between man and man." Thus, he was "predisposed to interpret economic and political problems in terms of moral principles." These moral qualities resided, not in the urban centers, which bred only social disorder, but among the "farmer stock" which possessed "the qualities on which this Nation has had to draw in order to meet every great crisis of the past." Agricultural life was the best means of obtaining that "bodily vigor" which produces "vigor of soul," and independent, property-owning farm families were the major source of social stability and the bulwark against internal conflict. For Roosevelt, with his interest in the out-of-doors, his emphasis on moral vigor arising from struggle with the elements, and his basic fear of social unrest, the good society was agrarian. He would have opposed bitterly any effort to turn back the industrial clock, yet his ultimate scheme of values was firmly rooted in an agrarian social order.

Roosevelt's emphasis on applied science and his conception of the good society as the classless agrarian society were contradictory trends of thought. The one, a faith which looked to the future, accepted wholeheartedly the basic elements of the new technology. The other, essentially backward-looking, longed for the simple agrarian Arcadia which, if it ever existed, could never be revived. He faced two directions at once, accepting the technical requirements of an increasingly organized industrial society, but fearing its social consequences. In this sense, and in this sense alone, Roosevelt sought Jeffersonian ends through Hamiltonian means. He had great respect for both men, each of whom manifested one side of his own contradictory nature. But he admired even more

Abraham Lincoln, the spokesman of the "plain people," whose life combined agrarian simplicity and national vigor. By the same token, Roosevelt considered his irrigation program as one of his administration's most important contributions. It expressed in concrete terms his own paradoxical nature: the preservation of American virtues of the past through methods abundantly appropriate to the present.

The contradictory elements of Roosevelt's outlook fused also in an almost mystical approach to the political order best described as "social atomism." Strongly affirming the beneficial role of both expert leadership and the vast mass of humanity, he could not fit into his scheme of things intervening group organization on the middle levels of power. Americans should live, he thought, as individuals rather than as members of "partial" groups, their loyalties should be given not to a class or section but to their national leader. As his administration encountered continued difficulty with Congress, Roosevelt relied more and more on executive commissions, and on action based upon the theory that the executive was the "steward" of the public interest. Feeling that he, rather than Congress, voiced most accurately the popular will, he advocated direct as opposed to representative government. Unable to adjust to a Congress which rejected his gospel of efficiency, Roosevelt took his case to the "people." In doing so he not only bypassed the lawmakers but also defied the group demands of organized American society. Growing ever more resentful of the hindrances of a Congress which expressed these demands, Roosevelt drew closer to a conception of the political organization of society wherein representative government would be minimized, and a strong leader, ruling through vigorous purpose, efficiency, and technology, would derive his support from a direct, personal relationship with the people.

As president, Roosevelt concentrated on problems which would not raise issues of internal social conflict—foreign policy and conservation. Increasingly stressing the conservation program during his second term of office, Roosevelt looked upon it as the most important contribution of his administration in domestic affairs. Conservation gave wide scope to government by experts, to investigation by commissions, to efficiency in planning and execution. It called forth patriotic sentiments which could override internal differences. More efficient production of material goods would help solve the labor problem in the way he thought it could be solved—by providing full employment and lower living costs. Even more important, through the federal irrigation program and the Country Life Movement, both of which Roosevelt encouraged, the President thought that he was buttressing the "Republic" in its most vital spot. Warning President-elect Taft that rural migration to cities would create a decline in the nation's population, in December 1908 Roosevelt urged his successor to formulate a program for country life improvement. "Among the various legacies of trouble which I leave you," he entreated, "there is none to which I more earnestly hope for your thought and care than this."

Herbert Croly's *The Promise of American Life,* written in 1908, articulated these tendencies in Roosevelt's political and social thought. Croly deeply feared that group consciousness in America would lead at best to an aimless, drifting society, and at worst to disastrous internal conflict. Vigorous, national purpose, he

argued, should replace the current American faith in automatic evolution
toward a better society. Less a blueprint than a simple plea for action,
The Promise of American Life immediately appealed to Roosevelt as the scholarly
expression of the assumptions upon which he had acted as president. And in
domestic affairs there was no better illustration of those assumptions than
the administration's conservation policies. Croly's work, the president declared,
was "the most profound and illuminating study of our national conditions which
has appeared for many years."

In holding these attitudes, Roosevelt personally embodied the popular
impulses which swung behind the conservation movement during the years of
the great crusade. That crusade found its greatest support among the American
urban middle class which shrank in fear from the profound social changes
being wrought by the technological age. These people looked backward to
individualist agrarian ideals, yet they approved social planning as a means to
control their main enemy—group struggle for power. A vigorous and purposeful
government became the vehicle by which ideals derived from an individualistic
society became adjusted to a new collective age. And the conservation movement
provided the most far-reaching opportunity to effect that adjustment. Herein
lay much of the social and cultural meaning of the movement for progressive
resource planning.

CONSERVATION AND THE GRASS ROOTS

The deepest significance of the conservation movement, however, lay in its
political implications: how should resource decisions be made and by whom?
Each resource problem involved conflicts. Should they be resolved through
partisan politics, through compromise among competing groups, or through
judicial decision? To conservationists such methods would defeat the inner spirit
of the gospel of efficiency. Instead, experts, using technical and scientific
methods, should decide all matters of development and utilization of resources,
all problems of allocation of funds. Federal land management agencies should
resolve land-use differences among livestock, wildlife, irrigation, recreation,
and settler groups. National commissions should adjust power, irrigation,
navigation, and flood control interests to promote the highest multiple-purpose
development of river basins. The crux of the gospel of efficiency lay in a
rational and scientific method of making basic technological decisions through
a single, central authority.

Resource users throughout the country differed sharply from this point of view.
They did not share the conservationists' desire for integrated planning and
central direction. Instead, each group considered its own particular interest as
far more important than any other. Resource users formed their opinions about
conservation questions within the limited experience of specific problems faced in
their local communities. They understood little and cared less for the needs of
the nation as a whole. This approach to resource affairs stood in direct contrast to
the over-all point of view of the conservationists. While the first gave rise to
centrifugal tendencies in resource management, the second produced centripetal
influences. While resource-use groups held a multitude of diverse aims which

stemmed from many limited and local experiences of particular problems, conservationists held comprehensive and unified objectives. An expert adjustment of resourse conflicts plainly would fulfill the broad objectives of conservation leaders, but it hardly sufficed to achieve the aims of particular localities more concerned with the problems which they knew firsthand.

Roosevelt conservation leaders had difficulty in adjusting these conflicting outlooks. Their entire program emphasized a flow of authority from the top down and minimized the political importance of institutions which reflected the organized sentiment of local communities. Pinchot and Roosevelt did take into account grass-roots interests, but only to facilitate administration and to prevent their decisions from arousing too much resentment. They postponed forest reserve executive orders until after elections, and cultivated the favor of stockmen to gain support for the transfer of the reserves to the Department of Agriculture. The Forest Service decentralized its administration so that federal officials could become better acquainted with local interests. Conservation leaders, however, rarely, if ever, permitted grass-roots groups to decide policy questions. These matters, they argued, could be left to local groups, or to political pressure in Congress only at the risk of "selling out" the national welfare to "special interests."

Grass-roots groups throughout the country had few positive objectives in common, but they shared a violent revulsion against the scientific, calculated methods of resource use adjustment favored by the conservationists. Both large and small property owners knew that the conservationists' plans involved methods of decision far beyond their control, and each group feared that a broader program would obscure its own specific needs or minimize its own project. Basin-wide river planning might require a dam in another locality. Multiple-purpose dams might provide less water desperately needed for navigation and more for electric power for some remote industry. Rigid grazing control might benefit the irrigator in the lower basin, but curtail the activities of stockmen on the headwaters. Each group desired financial and technical aid from the federal government, and each supported executive action when favorable to it, but none could feel a deep sense of participation in the process by which technical experts made resource decisions. Experience with the Forest Service and Bureau of Reclamation alienated many groups which found it difficult to influence administrative policy. They opposed plans to establish executive adjustment of conflicting uses and favored methods of decision over which they felt they had some measure of control.

Grass-roots groups utilized a variety of political methods, both judicial and legislative, to protect their interests. Through pressure on federal agencies or influence in selecting personnel, they could even modify the administrative process itself. Western water users, for example, resorted to the courts to counteract a rational state water law and efficient federal water development, both of which they viewed as a menace to their existing rights. The water laws proposed by Elwood Mead provided for administrative determination of available supplies and existing priorities, adjustment of present conflicts, and supervision of future filings. Fearing that their claims would suffer under this arrangement, water users preferred the older method of judicial determination of rights, a procedure in which they felt they had some degree of influence. Water users involved in interstate conflicts preferred to present their cases to the federal courts rather than to permit an administrative determination of rights which might follow the requirements of development rather than the merits of each individual claim.

Resource groups frequently obtained crucial influence with federal agencies which dealt with their problems. Not until 1913 did water users move into the inner circles of the Bureau of Reclamation, but after 1901 Western stockmen held a key position in the Forest Service. Using Albert Potter as his major contact with the grazers, Pinchot developed a close working arrangement with the large cattlemen to obtain their support for the transfer. Throughout the years before World War I the same group continued to support the Forest Service, through a tacit agreement that if federal officials would push a leasing program for the public domain, the cattlemen would not object to administrative grazing regulations. This happy arrangement then came to an end, as decisions to increase grazing fees and to reduce the number of livestock permitted in the forests both revealed the declining influence of the stockmen and precipitated their open hostility toward the Forest Service.

Nationwide pressure groups became the most effective technique adopted by resource users to influence resource decisions. Organizations such as the National Rivers and Harbors Congress, the American National Livestock Association, or the National Water Users Association grew up to represent the active segments of particular interests in their bid for influence in the conservation program. Although they quickly obtained political support from local congressmen, they remained thoroughly nonpartisan. Cooperating closely with congressional committees which dealt with special resource problems, each group bargained politically with others to obtain sufficient votes to pass its program. Through these logrolling techniques Congress developed many projects at once to satisfy a great number of localities rather than to construct the most important ones first. Through the same method it preferred to scatter appropriations over many projects to be spent year by year rather than to concentrate them on those developments most needed. These methods of national political organization and bargaining constituted the characteristic pattern of making resource decisions. Through them local groups achieved a sense of participation in and control over resource development which they did not receive from the more centrally directed methods of the conservationists.

Resource users played a fundamental role in shaping the character of development in a manner contrary to the aims of conservationists. They created a single, rather than a multiple-purpose attack on resource affairs. Economic organizations concerned with single interests—such as navigation, flood control, or irrigation—joined with administrative agencies in charge of individual programs and congressional committees which dealt with specialized subjects to defeat an integrated approach. Through policies devoted to the development of a single resource, Congress found protection against independent executive action, administrative agencies discovered a means to prevent coordination of their work with other bureaus, and local interests created programs of direct benefit to themselves and under their control. Private organizations and their congressional allies established this pattern. Although administrative agencies, such as the Corps of Engineers, took much initiative in preserving their administrative independence, their concern for single-purpose development reflected rather than molded the attitude of Congress. Single-purpose policies, impractical from the point of view of the conservation ideal of maximum development through scientific adjustment of competing uses, became the predominant pattern because they provided opportunities for grass-roots participation in decision-making. They enabled resource users to feel that they had some degree of control over policies that affected them.

The first American conservation movement experimented with the application of the new technology to resource management. Requiring centralized and coordinated decisions, however, this procedure conflicted with American political institutions which drew their vitality from filling local needs. This conflict between the centralizing tendencies of effective economic organization and the decentralizing forces inherent in a multitude of geographical interests presented problems to challenge even the wisest statesman. The Theodore Roosevelt administration, essentially hostile to the wide distribution of decision-making, grappled with this problem but failed to solve it. Instead of recognizing the paradoxes which their own approach raised, conservationists choose merely to identify their opposition as "selfish interests." Yet the conservation movement raised a fundamental question in American life: How can large-scale economic development be effective and at the same time fulfill the desire for significant grass-roots participation? How can the technical requirements of an increasingly complex society be adjusted to the need for the expression of partial and limited aims? This was the basic political problem which a technological age, the spirit of which the conservation movement fully embodied, bequeathed to American society.

four
from federal conservation policy, 1921–1933

DONALD C. SWAIN

One of the perennial problems of American historiography,
the extent to which progressivism persisted into the
1920s, has been illuminated by the work of Donald C.
Swain (b. 1931). In his book Federal Conservation Policy,
1921–1933 *(1963) he shows that it was exactly those*
elements of the conservation movement emphasized by
Hays that continued most successfully during the Republican
years of the nineteen-twenties. Swain received his doctorate
at the University of California, Berkeley, and since 1963
has taught at the University of California, Davis. He is
also the author of Wilderness Defender: Horace M.
Albright and Conservation *(1970).*

The personalities and political philosophies of three
Republican Presidents influenced federal resource programs
during the 1920's. Executive preference in matters of
policy created a milieu of voluntarism, "organized
coöperation," and decentralization in which the federal
conservation agencies often found it advantageous to soft
pedal resource regulation and to emphasize service functions.
Warren G. Harding and Calvin Coolidge, while paying
scant attention to conservation policy, tended to inhibit

Source: Donald C. Swain, *Federal Conservation Policy, 1921–1933*
(Berkeley: University of California Press, 1963), pp. 160–70.
Originally published by the University of California Press;
reprinted by permission of The Regents of the University of
California.

positive federal conservation activity. Herbert Hoover, on the other hand, demonstrated throughout the 1920's an active and constructive interest in promoting national conservation programs.

Riding to office on a wave of reaction against wartime restrictions, Harding understood little of the necessity for conserving natural resources. In his view, the conservation issue was unimportant. He stood for rapid resource development within an unfettered private enterprise system. Albert B. Fall, his Secretary of the Interior, symbolized the extent to which the Republican President at first ignored conservation considerations. Shortly before his death, however, Harding began to realize the importance of conserving national resources. On his return voyage from Alaska in 1923, he instructed Hoover to rough out a speech for him on Alaskan resource policy. After introducing "his usual three-dollar words and sonorous phrases," he delivered the address, and as one conservationist observed, "Gifford Pinchot himself never packed more conservation into a single speech." Thus, when his death occurred, Harding was perhaps on the verge of taking a strong conservation position. Unfortunately, he had already initiated an era of executive laxity during which high federal officials were free to undermine strict resource regulation. The Teapot Dome scandal, eventuating from the President's own lack of interest in resource administration, is the best example. Without vigorous executive support, the conservation bureaus had to fall back on voluntary programs designed, in general, to appease industrial and commercial interests.

Succeeding to the presidency in 1923, Calvin Coolidge interested himself primarily in trimming the federal budget while largely ignoring natural resources. The era of executive laxity continued. The Man from Vermont represented the "genius of the average," as one benevolent critic put it. He had almost no aptitude for the subtleties of conservation policy. And his failure to grasp the long-range implications of resource problems might have proved disastrous. It was monumental naïveté, for example, to compare Muscle Shoals in value to a "first class battleship." With evident pride, he considered himself a "practical" man. But his emphasis on economy in governmental expenditures was impractical in the long run. Among other things it severely hampered the federal conservation program. Hoover remarked later about Coolidge's reluctance "to undertake much that was new or cost money." Although the New Englander promoted coöperative policies in forestry, wildlife, and recreation, his only important influence on conservation came as a result of his insistence on decentralization. He wanted the states to discharge their public functions "so faithfully that instead of an extension on the part of the Federal Government there can be a contraction." When translated into action at the bureau level, this dictum meant less power for the federal conservation agencies, who were expected to stimulate state supervision of resources whenever possible.

II

Herbert Hoover, in contrast to his immediate predecessors, was a key conservation figure. As Secretary of Commerce, he exerted a large influence in the affairs of both the Harding and Coolidge administrations, demonstrating his personal

interest in resource policy-making. From his cabinet office in Washington
he crusaded for such conservation causes as the regulation of Alaskan salmon
fisheries, the control of water pollution, the establishment of fish nurseries,
construction of a St. Lawrence waterway, the improvement of inland navigation,
and the authorization of the Boulder Canyon project. Once in the White
House, he concentrated on flood control, waterways development, and oil
conservation. That he was a sincere conservationist is beyond question.

The methods by which he chose to implement his conservation ideas remained
open to criticism. Believing wholeheartedly that natural resources should not
be plundered in the name of individualism, he was nevertheless an individualist.
How to reconcile his conservation thinking with his individualistic philosophy,
therefore, became his personal dilemma. His attempts to solve that dilemma
resulted in vigorous programs to reduce waste, to promote coöperation,
and to decentralize conservation controls.

Hoover's campaigns against waste and, conversely, for efficiency developed
into one of the high lights of the early 1920's. He plugged incessantly
for progressive industrial technology and increased scientific research, enlarging
the scientific work of the Department of Commerce as a public example.
He formed trade associations and arranged voluntary industrial liaisons in which
he preached national efficiency at every opportunity. His ideas unquestionably
influenced his contemporaries. And the logic of his position led him into
conservation. Yet, in regard to the elimination of waste, one may legitimately
inquire whether Hoover's primary concern was to conserve natural resources or
to stimulate ever greater production. With some inconsistency, both
considerations figured prominently in his thinking. Frequently the latter
seemed to be the more important.

His quest for efficiency, moreover, led him into the difficult area of
governmental reorganization. Attacking the multidepartmental conservation
set-up of the federal government, he called for a unification of conservation
bureaucracy. He suggested that Congress establish a new organization, grouping
resource agencies according to their major purposes. Yet he confined his interest
in reorganization almost entirely to administration and methodology. To him,
it seemed, conservation results loomed less important than conservation
organization. Still, his strong belief in organizational continuity motivated
him to appoint the heads of scientific bureaus exclusively from within the
bureaus themselves, a policy which had important implications for the federal
conservation program.

Hoover championed voluntarism as the method by which the federal
government could achieve regulatory results without circumscribing the individual
rights. Styling his approach as "Organized Coöperation," he sought to
persuade states and individuals to coöperate with the federal government in
order to reach certain goals. Even before he became President, his ideas about
coöperation permeated the federal establishment. The Forest Service, the
Bureau of Fisheries, the Army Engineers, the Biological Survey, the Bureau of
Mines, and the Geological Survey all resorted to policies of coöperation
during the 'twenties. Later, when Hoover became Chief Executive, he sought
assiduously to avoid federal regulation. "Only when voluntary action wholly

failed," officials of his administration have reported, "was Hoover prepared to undertake [direct] governmental action." In certain instances he achieved considerable success by means of coöperation; his oil policy is a good example. But on the whole, coöperative tactics failed in the face of strong opposition from resource users. By the time of the New Deal, the policy of coöperation stood generally discredited. Because of his commitment to rugged individualism, Hoover never fully realized the significance to conservation of strong and direct government regulation.

Another characteristic Hoover response during the 1920's was decentralization. Influenced here more than elsewhere by the Republican Party, he consistently advocated states rights and state responsibilities. "To sustain the spirit of responsibility of States, of municipalities, of industry and the community at large," he stated in 1930, "is the one safeguard against overwhelming centralization and degeneration of that independence and initiative which are the very foundations of democracy." Hoover's penchant for decentralized organization had a direct effect on his conservation thinking. It caused him to attempt a bold new policy toward the public domain, the range lands of which stood in need of attention.

III

The arid and semiarid lands of the West, comprising nearly one-third of the total area of the United States, form a valuable natural range for domestic livestock. By the decade of the 'twenties the federal government, true to its easy land policy, had sold the best sections of this vast domain to private individuals and landholding corporations. The government still owned more than 186,000,000 acres of range land, a fact which made it the largest landlord in the West. Despite their lack of title to the land, ranchers and stockmen had become accustomed to free use of these publicly owned areas. Occasionally they claimed exclusive jurisdiction over certain pastures. The trouble was that while supplementary forage on the public domain often became essential to successful grazing operations, the stockmen overused the range. They had little real chance to preserve natural vegetation because the competitive race for free forage forced them to put cattle onto the ranges too early in the spring and encouraged a continual overgrazing. After a time the native grasses tended to disappear, replaced by less desirable varieties or by total barrenness. The Forest Service had brought range lands within the national forests under regulation, but grazers still abused and exploited the unregulated public domain. After conservation organizations made repeated attempts to institute a grazing permit system for the public lands without success, Hoover decided to attack this persistent problem.

In August, 1929 he dispatched a message to the Conference of Western Governors stating his general objectives.

. . . it is my desire [he wrote] to work out more constructive policies for consideration in our grazing lands, our water storage, and our mineral resources, at the same time check the growth of Federal

*bureaucracy, reduce Federal interference in affairs of essentially local
interest, and thereby increase the opportunity of the states to govern
themselves, and in all obtain better government.*

As was his custom, he proposed a joint commission to study the problem. The
governors agreed to coöperate, and Congress authorized the commission in
April, 1930. Chaired by James R. Garfield, Secretary of the Interior under
Theodore Roosevelt, and including William B. Greeley, former Forester, the
Committee on the Conservation and Administration of the Public Domain
commanded respect. Its report of early 1931 reflected Hoover's great influence.
It proposed to place the unreserved and unappropriated public domain under
responsible administration "for the conservation and beneficial use of its
resources." The federal government, it suggested, should maintain jurisdiction
over all reclamation projects, national forests, national parks and monuments,
wildlife refuges, and any area important to the national defense. The remaining
public holdings, valuable primarily as range land, were to be granted to the
states. The public ranges within states not wishing to accept such a grant,
the report continued, should be placed under federal regulation. The committee
recommended, finally, that the national government pass title to public
mineral lands to the states, with the reservation that federal agencies continue
to hold the mineral rights. Supported fiercely by the Hoover administration, these
proposals nevertheless had no chance of legislative enactment. A sincere
attempt to bring effective regulation to the public domain, the plan satisfied
too few people.

Conservationists disapproved of Hoover's suggestions for two main reasons.
The Roosevelt-Pinchot faction would not sanction the reversal of a principle
for which they had fought so hard—federal regulation of the resources of the
public domain. Other conservation advocates believed the states incapable
of coping with such a large regulatory problem. In the final analysis, the states
themselves had little to gain by the committee's proposals. Regulating
the public ranges would be a colossal headache, and state governments did
not want title to mineral lands so long as the mineral rights resided in the
federal government.

In spite of the failure of Hoover's plan for the public domain, his efforts
produced a significant negative result. By offering the public lands to the states,
and having the states reject the offer, the federal government freed itself to
proceed with its own methods of regulation. The states-rights argument, which
recurred periodically during grazing and mineral controversies, lost its
validity. With the states refusing to act, the federal government had no
alternative but to assume responsibility for grazing regulation. The quibbling
over methods of range administration had not ended, but the argument over
jurisdiction ceased. In 1934 the Taylor Grazing Act—although less than
ideal legislation—at last brought conservation regulation to the public ranges
of the West.

Hoover's emphasis on decentralization disappointed many conservationists who
had hoped for a resurgence of strong and direct federal conservation

participation. The old Progressive conservationists, still greatly influenced by Gifford Pinchot, were particularly disenchanted with Hoover.

*Instead of being inspired, [one of them wrote] as I had hoped and
believed, by a perception of the immense gains to the public welfare
that might be realized by applying science, expert knowledge, the
engineer's viewpoint, and the principles of business efficiency
to the task of making government serve the multitudinous and complex
requirements of a highly organized modern world, I believe he
[Hoover] draws back in apprehension of what looks to him like an
eventual Frankenstein. . . .*

IV

During the era of Hoover's national prominence a curious ambivalence characterized his thinking about natural resources. A convert to the conservation philosophy, he was plagued by personal inconsistencies. He announced early in his administration that "conservation of natural resources is a fixed policy of the government," but he refused to pursue certain conservation projects because he objected to their political or economic implications. He became a pioneer advocate of watershed planning, yet he vehemently rejected the idea of comprehensive federal development of Muscle Shoals. He proposed to bring the public domain under regulation, but the method he chose foredoomed his plan to failure. Although he realized fully the imperative of restricting the national production of petroleum, he stubbornly eschewed direct federal intervention. Torn between conservation considerations and strict individualism, he could not bring himself to compromise his individualistic philosophy. He was thus less effective in implementing his conservation plans than he himself had hoped to be. As the first conservationist President since Theodore Roosevelt, Hoover had aroused expectations among conservation partisans. He failed to fulfill their high hopes. His primary contribution, achieved in spite of a severe economic depression, was to rekindle national interest in the orderly development of natural resources. During his administration the era of executive laxity ended. In his hands, the presidency once more became a constructive force in the campaign to conserve public resources. Hoover prepared the way for some of the dramatic conservation successes of Franklin Roosevelt by renewing the image of the President as a conservation leader.

V

Regardless of executive laxity, the federal conservation bureaus achieved important conservation successes during the 1920's, under Harding, Coolidge, and Hoover, demonstrating a significant bureaucratic continuity. Led by scientists or scientifically trained specialists, these bureaus carried out their day-to-day conservation functions, on the whole, with commendable skill. Even the weaker agencies such as the Biological Survey, the Bureau of Reclamation, the Geological Survey, and the Bureau of Mines accomplished significant conservation results. Their weaknesses fell mainly in the area of leadership. When the federal bureaucracy functions up to capacity, it formulates plans, delineates program requirements, and works mightily to obtain congressional approval for them. During the 1920's the less effective conservation bureaus either failed to propose viable resource programs or refused to press their legislative demands in Congress. The strong conservation agencies, on the other hand, such as the Forest Service and the National Park Service, consistently displayed bureaucratic imagination and drive. Truly dedicated to conserving natural resources, these two federal bureaus matured specific resource plans and invariably secured appropriate legislation from Congress. The key to their success was organizational continuity and above-average personnel.

Both of these agencies believed thoroughly in promotion from within. Young men coming into the Forest Service or the Park Service could look forward, after a time, to positions of responsibility in their bureaus. When President Hoover adopted the merit system of internal promotion for all the federal technical agencies, he assured scientific competence. But more important—in a manner which Hoover did not suspect—his promotion policy insured Progressive-minded leadership for many of the conservation bureaus. With merit rather than politics as the guide to promotion, men who had originally joined resource bureaus during the early stages of the Roosevelt-Pinchot conservation movement, or shortly before, moved steadily into positions of bureaucratic leadership. R. Y. Stuart of the Forest Service entered the Department of Agriculture in 1906 and became a close associate of Gifford Pinchot. Although he took a leave of absence from the Forest Service in the early 1920's to work in the Pennsylvania forestry commission, Stuart was clearly a product of the federal bureaucracy. He came to office in 1928. Horace M. Albright, Director of the National Park Service, first joined the Department of the Interior in 1914. An acknowledged Progressive, he assumed bureau leadership in 1929. Walter C. Mendenhall, of the Geological Survey, began his government service in 1894, at the very beginning of the conservation surge. He took charge of his bureau in 1930. Henry O'Malley, of the Bureau of Fisheries, head of that agency from 1921 to 1933, initially associated himself with the government in 1897. Paul G. Redington became chief of the Biological Survey in 1927 after a twenty-three year apprenticeship in the Forest Service. Hugh Bennett, appointed to the Soil Survey in 1903, assumed command of the federal soil conservation program in 1930. E. A. Sherman, Raphael Zon, Earle H. Clapp, and F. A. Silcox of the Forest Service hierarchy all entered civil service between 1903 and 1907. William B. Greeley and Stephen T. Mather, important bureau chiefs in the years immediately before Hoover's administration, were both Bull Moose sympathizers. Powerful throughout the 1920's, conservationists nurtured during the Progressive era became more and more influential in the bureaucracy as the decade concluded. Hoover's promotion policy allowed them to entrench their influence, not only in the Forest Service and the Park Service, but in many other federal conservation agencies as well. The zeal of these men may well explain the achievements of the federal conservation and which it becomes the Representatives of a wise and free people to afford—especially our University at Cambridge, founded by the wisdom and virtue of our ancestors, approved by long experience of its utility, and honoured by the many illustrious characters which have adorned our country, and who imbibe the first principles of science at that pure and copious fountain.

Nor can the schools throughout this Commonwealth be permitted to continue under such inattention and discouragement as they have for many years suffered, to the irreparable injury of the present and future generation, and to the indelible disgrace of a free government. We shall therefore hold ourselves obliged to form proper establishments for restoring them to their primitive dignity and usefulness.

It gives us singular pleasure to find the Society of Arts, &c. lately founded in this Commonwealth, dignified and enriched by the addition of many respectable literary characters, and promising such happy improvement. . . Institutions, which have a tendency "To cherish the interests of literature and sciences, to extend and improve commerce, to promote agriculture, arts, trades, and manufactures, and a natural history of the country," are by the Constitution intituled to, and cannot fail to find the patronage and protection of the Government.

We beg leave to assure your Excellency that we shall make it our sincere endeavour, both by precept and example, to countenance and inculcate obedience to the laws, with the principles of religion, patriotism, "Humanity, and general benevolence, public and private charity, industry and frugality, honesty and punctuality in dealing, sincerity, good humour, and all social affections, and generous sentiments among the people."

And as the dignity and reputation of the Commonwealth, as well as the interest of the subjects, demand the independence both of the Chief Magistrate and of the Justices of the Supreme Judicial Court, so it shall be among our first Acts of Legislation, to provide and establish permenant and honorable salaries for each.

May it please your Excellency,

With all the liberality and candor, unanimity and harmony which can consist with the due exercise of the powers and rights vested in the several branches respectively, We shall now proceed to the business of the session, and shall forthwith attend to the revision of the laws and to the framing such new Statutes as may be requisite for accomplishing the important purpose of our election; and shall at all times pay that respect to the communications and recommendation[s] of your Excellency, and give the dispach to the public business which the safety and happiness of the commonwealth may require.

69. Samuel Adams: "This great Business was carried through with good Humour among the People."

[Samuel Adams to John Adams, Philadelphia, July 10, 1780, Harry Alonzo Cushing, ed., *The Writings of Samuel Adams* (New York, 1908), IV, 199-200]

MY DEAR SIR

I wrote to you several Times when I was at Boston, and receivd your Favor by the Marquis de la Fayette. Another, to which you referrd me, has not yet come to hand. This Letter will be deliverd to you by Mr Searle, a Member of Congress for the State of Pennsylvania. He will be better able to inform you of the State of things here, than I can, who after twelve Months Absence from this City, returnd but a few days ago. The People of Massachusetts have at length agreed to the Form of a civil Constitution, in Nothing varying from a Copy which I sent to you by a Son of our Friend General Warren. This great Business was carried through with much good Humour among the People, and even in Berkshire, where some Persons led us to expect it would meet with many Obstructions. Never was a good Constitution more wanted than at this Juncture. Among other more lasting Advantages, I hope that in Consequence of it, the Part which that State must take in the War, will be conducted with greater Attention and better Effect. Who is to be the first Man, will be determind in September, when if our News papers rightly inform us, the new Government is to take Place. The Burden will fall on the Shoulders of one of two Gentlemen whom you know. May Heaven lead the People to the wisest Choice. The first chosen Governor may probably have it in his Power to do more good or more Hurt than any of his successors. The french Fleet is not yet arrivd. Perhaps their long Passage may turn out for the best. An earlier Arrival might have found us not altogether prepared to cooperate with them to the best Advantage. I now think we shall be ready to joyn them. One would think the Exertion which America might make with such Aid, would rid us of British Barbarians. I hope this will be a vigorous and an effective Campaign. I left Massachusetts exceedingly active in filling up their Battalions by Drafts, besides raising 4000 Militia for the Service.

Mr Laurens arrivd here from the Southward a few Days past. He will speedily embark for Holland to prosecute a Business which you are not unacquainted with. Adieu my dear Sir.

Y^r affectionate Friend

program, 1921 to 1933. Their presence, moreover, smoothed the transition from Hoover to Roosevelt and keyed the favorable bureaucratic response to New Deal conservation planning.

VI

Science had become increasingly important in the federal establishment during the 'twenties. Following the budgetary cut-backs of the post-World War I years, Congress showed a willingness to underwrite federal research programs on a greatly expanded basis. Influenced by the example of private industry, the lawmakers found scientific research increasingly respectable. Their authorization of the comprehensive river-basin surveys by the Army Engineers was the beginning of a new epoch in conservation science. The year 1926 to 1927 seemed to mark the turning point. As demonstrated earlier, the Forest Service, the Bureau of Fisheries, the Bureau of Mines, the Geological Survey, and the Bureau of Chemistry and Soils, all received somewhat enlarged research appropriations after 1927. At about the same time, a new scientific interest emerged in the National Park Service and in the Bureau of Reclamation. The general trend of federal conservation practice was to turn to science as the basis for resource policy.

Gaining stature with their research programs, government scientists increased their bureaucratic influence. In 1927, for example, the hierarchy of the Department of the Interior, which had frequently been less than enthusiastic about science, stated officially that "The first essential to efficient administration of a conservation policy is knowledge—detailed information as to what the natural resources are and where they are to be found." Moreover, energized by scientists, certain conservation bureaus fought successfully for expanded basic research. "There can be no applied science," the Director of the Geological Survey wrote in 1928, "unless there is science to apply. The application of science . . . depends upon the maintenance of research that discovers new facts and new natural laws that can be put to use." The Geological Survey, indeed, secured a series of handsome appropriations for basic research in 1930 to 1933. Then the depression hit and Congress began slashing research funds. Yet the conservation bureaus, with great confidence in the attractiveness of government science, stood their ground. In the face of economic collapse, the Bureau of Chemistry and Soils, for instance, called for more, not less, scientific research. The investigative programs of the resource bureaus shrank after 1932, but not as much as many of their other functions.

By the end of Hoover's administration federally supported scientific and technologic research had become more important than ever before. Capitalizing on the generosity of Congress, the conservation bureaus accumulated a large amount of valuable resource data. Soil erosion research progressed so rapidly, for example, that by 1933 Hugh Bennett had the scientific information on which to build his Soil Conservation Service. The Bureau of Fisheries, undertaking a wide range of scientific projects, greatly enlarged its knowledge of the life habits of fishes and made significant advances in the study of fish diseases. The Bureau of Mines perfected important new techniques of mineral extraction and refining, achieving striking technological successes. The Forest Service officially embraced science as the essential preliminary to policy-making. Its nation-wide timber survey, its forest products research, and its studies of forest management improved prospects for increased timber production and decreased timber waste. Even the Army Engineers rose to scientific heights with their excellent investigations of American river basins. By 1933 the federal conservation bureaus had collected the body of data which served as the scientific basis for New Deal resource planning. During the late 1920's government scientists were able to institutionalize a powerful reliance on scientific research. The example of the conservation agencies added impetus to the trend which, in the 1930's, saw research itself win recognition as a national resource. Considerably before the second Roosevelt entered the White House, science and technology had become dominant in resource decisions at the bureau level.

The acceptance of the principle of multiple-purpose resource planning went hand in hand with increased federal reliance on science. The logical use of resource data was developmental planning. As the prestige of research agencies mounted, and as research findings proved more and more valuable in conserving resources, Congress began to lean in the direction of the multiple-purpose approach. In matters of water development, the idea of watershed or river basin planning gained surprisingly wide acceptance. In agriculture, forestry, and soil conservation the concept of planned land utilization became progressively more important. By the time of the New Deal, resource planning had clearly become respectable. Agriculturists had already begun to think in terms of removing farmers from submarginal lands by a "resettlement" process. Congress had already committed itself to the multiple-purpose development of the Muscle Shoals region. Consequently, the Resettlement Administration and the Tennessee Valley Authority followed naturally from pressures which began building before the advent of the New Deal.

The aesthetic conservationists, whom Pinchot had deplored as "nature lovers," gained both strength and prestige during the 1920's. As the National Park Service coalesced and expanded, it furnished the organizational focus for an aesthetic renaissance and for a resurgence of preservationism. Long ignored in national conservation policy, wildlife protection and the preservation of natural beauty became popular causes. Challenging the utilitarians openly and aggressively, aesthetic conservationists forced their powerful opponents to recognize the desirability of protecting certain forms of animal life and to acknowledge the necessity for preserving unique areas of natural beauty. On the rise throughout the decade, "nature lovers" won equality within conservation ranks and received important support at the federal level.

VII

In spite of occasional lapses in federal leadership, the 1920's were productive years in the conservation of natural resources. Stimulated by a heterogeneous group of conservationists, politicians, and resource administrators, the federal government led the way to important conservation achievement. Nation-wide forest fire protection became a reality. Federal soil conservation work began. The Boulder Canyon project, first federally sponsored large-scale multiple-purpose river basin development, won authorization. Giant flood control programs for the Mississippi Valley and other rivers took form. An integrated system of inland waterways intersected the great central section of the United States. The generation of hydroelectric power for the first time received careful consideration in resource planning. A network of migratory bird sanctuaries materialized. The national parks became a great American institution, preserving magnificent natural scenes for the edification of future generations. Left without a dynamic national conservation leader throughout most of the 'twenties, the conservation bureaus carried on unobtrusively and, in general, effectively. They laid foundations for subsequent New Deal conservation achievements. Congress, too, chartered an independent course. Moving largely against the wishes of the Republican chief executives, the federal legislature had by 1933 anticipated the direction of much New Deal conservation policy. Contrary to widely held opinion, the national conservation program did not deteriorate in the 1920's. It expanded and matured.

five
conservation in
1952

STEPHEN RAUSHENBUSH

*Unlike the previous authors, all of whom have been
academic historians, Stephen Raushenbush wrote primarily
as an expert bureaucrat who dealt professionally with
resource policy. From an historical perspective, he
attempted to assess the present weakness and future
hopes of a conservation movement caught between a
developing American empire abroad and the domestic
priorities of the Truman administration at home. After
serving as a senior resource economist with the United
States Department of the Interior from 1937 to 1947,
Raushenbush became a consultant to the Public Affairs
Institute. Among his writings are* Our Conservation Job
(1949), Conserving and Developing Our Natural Resources
(1950), and Better Conservation Work *(1952).*

Conservation is in danger of becoming a lost cause.

As a cause, rather than a series of techniques, it started
with two ideas. The first was the concept of a national
patrimony, a God-given heritage and legacy which was to be
handled by responsible stewards rather than by prodigal
and wastrel sons. The second was that the advantages of our
natural resources should be shared by all the citizens of
the nation, not used primarily for the benefit of a few.

Today the emotional content of these old ideas survives
mainly among the small farmers who love the land which
gives them their living. It is their group of soil
conservationists that holds that "the right to own carries
the duty to conserve." But for most of the rest of the

Source: Stephen Raushenbush, "Conservation in 1952," *The
Annals of the American Academy of Political and Social Science*
281 (May 1952): 1–9. Reprinted by permission of the author
and the publisher.

community, the two moving ideas of Theodore Roosevelt, Gifford Pinchot, and the host of great conservationists of the early part of the century seem to have lost attractiveness. The cause that rose from these ideas has been weakened. This is not to say that many things are not still done in the name of conservation. It is not to say that there are few sincere recreationists, or few people worried about the pressure of population on land, or few diligent technicians of soil and forest conservation. They are all present. They are all doing valuable jobs of sorts. They are simply no longer so sure of their community of interest or so confident of the national value of their work as were the old-time leaders.

CONTRARY FORCES

What happened? Some five distinguishable forces and events battered away at the old ideal.

First was the peculiar sequence of war-depression-war-defense that has extended over the past 38 years. The war and defense periods drained our resources at rates that were unthought of in the early conservation days. In those emergencies there was little possibility of considering slower rates of use. The greatest service to future generations seemed clearly to be that of mobilizing all our resources as rapidly as possible. Sandwiched between war emergencies was an agricultural, coal, and lumber depression that began in the middle 1920's. Owners and tenants had to exploit the land, the forests, and the coal in destructive ways to stay alive. They had few funds to maintain the national resource capital. Dust storms then transported topsoil from the Midwest to Washington, and a few starts were made (the Civilian Conservation Corps and the Soil Conservation Service) toward belated conservation; but then war and defense claimed the national surplus. In this whole sequence of war-depression-war-defense it became easier to preach conservation than to achieve it, and easier to ignore it than to preach it.

Second was the demonstration of the ability of our applied scientists to produce substitutes or find alternate sources. When lumber became scarce, light metals and useful clay products were available. When good range for our sheep became scarce, synthetic substitutes for wool appeared. As the soil resources were depleted or eroded, a host of seed, insecticide, and fertilizer improvements produced larger crops on less land. Internal combustion engines made land available that had previously been used for the maintenance of horses and mules. When the more easily discovered petroleum resources approached exhaustion, new geophysical devices led to the discovery of other supplies. The popular faith now is that science will do everything for us, including the saving of our energy for more important purposes than the conservation of natural resources.

Third was the discovery that our exhaustible resources (conspicuously petroleum and high-grade iron ore) could be supplemented expeditiously and economically from abroad. The Rockefeller Board's report in 1950, *Partners in Progress,* pointed out that our heavy industry was dependent on imports for most of fifteen basic raw materials. It recommended American aid for development of these foreign necessities. We could become another England, importing raw materials, fabricating them, and exporting finished goods.

Not only did other world resources become available to us, while our financial position made it quite possible for us to obtain them on favorable terms, but international trade became more clearly a good and desirable thing. As a minor corollary, conservation of domestic resources in the sense of slower use, or use for higher-value purposes, seemed to become less important for our survival, or even, at the worst, another interference with international trade, world stability, and possibly peace.

Next was the fact that the nation experienced a fairly high standard of living, and during the past ten years an extremely high one, in spite of all the conservation failures and the heavy resource drains for war and defense. Prices of natural resources rose—some of them conspicuously above the general level—but increased incomes absorbed them without very much trouble, and were still high. These higher resource prices did not take us out of world markets for our finished goods. The organization and ownership of some resources became somewhat more concentrated; special tax privileges had to be given in order to induce oil and other mineral discoveries. Still, the benefits of the whole economic arrangement were largely shared—if not directly, then indirectly.

In the face of this situation, attention to the dark warnings of the prophets of shortages of land, oil, coking coal, and metals, of monopoly and of lower living standards, seemed both postponable and shiftable to those obviously benighted areas where population was more clearly pressing on resources.

It was only when the floods came roaring down the Missouri or the Kansas or the Ohio, or when material shortages inflated world prices disastrously, or when the threat of losing Middle Eastern oil resources appeared, that we had cause to remember the black prophecies. And these occasions did not come often. By and large, the people of the nation seem to have done extremely well, in spite of some serious neglects of the future and an accumulation of local ghost towns, eroded areas, and inflationary pressures circling out from raw materials.

Finally, the conservation ideal ran afoul of the fear that it might lead to too much governmental control. Even those who recognized clearly that the interests of time and society were not necessarily identical with the operations of the free market could also see that governmental action was not always a perfect solvent.

QUESTIONS OF FACT

The impact of these five happenings has been heightened by a number of disturbing questions about fact. The estimate of the United States Bureau of Mines that our coal reserves would last for many hundreds of years has been questioned in terms of the high costs of producing most of the reserves. Its figures that gasoline can be produced from coal at a cost of 14 cents a gallon have been challenged by the assertion of various industry groups that it may cost several times that much. The figures of the United States Forest Service indicating that our lumber and pulp supply is already inadequate for our needs and is growing more inadequate have been questioned sharply by the wood industries. The estimate of the Soil Conservation Service that we need to restore or rebuild several hundred million acres of rapidly or slowly eroding land has been doubted by technicians who put their trust in the methods by which production could be increased on the remaining land base. The United States Weather Bureau has expressed public doubts about the value of much of the cloud seeding that is now being undertaken in the arid West.

The confusion has been increased by the absence, from the end of World War I onward, of any common grouping of the various conservation interests. The conservation movement, like so much else in modern society, has been atomized. There are many separate groups, each devoted to some special purpose. But there has not been any inclusive association that attempted to find the similarities of all the resource situations, think out the major problems, and deal with them, or even to keep track of what were facts and what were special pleadings, and inform the public accordingly.

PAST AND PRESENT

To explain why conservation today is not quite so appealing a cause as it was in the first decade of the century is not to question the two ideas of wise use of a national patrimony and wide distribution of the benefits of that use. Those ideas are necessary for a nation that intends to survive and for a society that wishes to become a community. We shall come back to them in due time.

That time may come sooner than we now think. The scars left by the depression of the 1930's are so deep that it is hard for us to comprehend that we not only are out of it, but shall probably not again see anything of its magnitude of severity in our lifetime. Instead, we shall more probably see the growing population, the increasing demand, and the generally rising prices that can call for emergency conservation practices, as well as enable the resource owners to undertake them.

What the nation did for the major resource industries during the depression was conservation only in the life-saving sense, not in the sense of assuring stabilization of the land or forest base, or less wasteful physical recovery of minerals. The petroleum industry was allowed to step a little outside of the free market system by state-approved limitations of production. The agricultural industry moved out of it along the more difficult road of taxpayers' help to take surpluses off the market, the coal industry temporarily by a minimum price arrangement, and the forest industries, briefly under the National Recovery Administration, by price maintenance.

It was recognized at that time that many small farmers, coal mine operators, oil producers, and lumber companies were, in effect, outside of the business system. They could hardly be expected to act with foresight. They were not institutionally equipped to fend for themselves. They did not evaluate their own labor or their family labor at the market rate, nor withhold their products until price justified their efforts. They sought to maximize their incomes by maximizing production, gutted their resources in that endeavor, and were overwhelmed by the consequent glut. They had no credit resources to do otherwise. The social costs of overcutting and soil mining were loaded off onto their downstream neighbors, and later onto the general taxpayers.

The national consent that was given for these various breaks with the free market system did, along with other factors, result in higher incomes for resource owners, and these were recognized as a prerequisite for conservation. The gains to society from these actions became clear as the war and postwar demands grew. However, the gains could have been greater if good conservation practices had been a basic rather than a perfunctory part of the process of consent.

Since those days a considerable amount of conservation work has been done. It looks small against the backlog of things undone, but it is promising, in parts. The Southeast, for example, is a much greener and more prosperous-looking place than it was twenty or more years ago when it was still in the cotton rut. A large number of Soil Conservation Districts have been formed, and many of these are getting some work underway. The Bureau of Reclamation is saving a considerable number of older irrigation districts that have overused their water supplies. The United States Forest Service and the Bureau of Land Management have been able to make a small start on reseeding some of the public range. The Soil Conservation Service has at long last been able to undertake work on a dozen smaller watercourses.

All this is a fair start, but when it is put next to figures for private and public investment that may go as high as $25 billion for forest and soil work, $10 billion for reclamation work, and $60 billion for water control work, it looks small and inadequate.

NEEDS, PRICES, EFFICIENCY

Conservationists are bedeviled by three main questions whenever they look at that backlog. The first is, How is the national need to be met at reasonable prices when resource owners (particularly the small ones) refuse or are unable to adopt good conservation practices and the higher immediate costs that attend them? The answer found in the wood industries seems to be that it is not so to be met. The United States Forest Service finds that the cutting practices are still bad on about 60 per cent of the private forest land, and that the supply will be much less than the demand at reasonable prices for many generations to come. In addition, the social costs of clear-cutting, in the form of erosion and downstream flood damages, are still largely paid by others. The United States Forest Service has suggested state control, but if that fails, federal control, of cutting practices and reforestation. The woodworkers and the Congress of Industrial Organizations think federal control of both is necessary. The lumber and pulp industries oppose both suggestions. There has been almost no major public discussion of the matter in Congress for almost a decade.

The second question is, How can the governmental part of the conservation job be done efficiently? It was to this question that the Hoover Commission and the Cooke Commission (Water Resources Policy Commission) largely addressed themselves. The former aimed its heaviest guns at the competition between the Army Engineers and the Bureau of Reclamation in the Missouri Basin. It

recommended uniting them into one agency to get rid of a rivalry which
was carried on at the expense of the conservation ideas. Hardly was the ink dry
on its report before the Department of Agriculture produced a conservation
program of its own for the Missouri Basin. Without saying so, that report
indicated a belief that hardly any of the basic soil and forest conservation work
that was needed would be covered by the other agencies. Another $4 billion
of private and public investment was required to meet those needs in addition to
the water control projects (which may cost $6 billion) already authorized by
Congress.

Considerable emphasis was added to this second question as a result of the
Kansas and Osage River floods of 1951. For almost the first time, the people of
the region who were interested in upstream conservation protested the emphasis
laid on, and the money to be committed to, large flood-protection dams that
did little or nothing for the farmers and upstream communities. The connection
between forest and soil conservation and downstream water control had
rarely been clearer. It was also the burden of the two thousand pages of the
Cooke Commission's report: only in unified watershed work was there any
efficiency, any maximizing of social benefits.

Another part of the answer may well lie in government aid in establishing
credit facilities for small owners, that are tailored to the needs of soil,
forest, and water conservation.

FOR WHOSE BENEFIT?

The third question is, For whose benefit should national aid to conservation and
development be undertaken? This presents itself for answer in several forms.
One of them relates to the big cities that have expanded into the natural
flood plains of the rivers. Now they want their buildings in those flood plains
protected at national expense. The more they have expanded into them,
the more money they need. Every extra group of buildings in the flood plains
becomes a justification for extra hundreds of thousands of dollars of flood
control works—a fact which explains part of the $60 billion figure for future
water control. To some conservationists this seems like putting a reward
on carelessness. Should the process be allowed to go on? Should this aid be
given free, or should the cities pay part of the costs? The corollary questions are
underlined by the probability that Congress will, in our time, never have
unlimited funds, and that each protective measure is at the expense of
some other one, elsewhere.

The question also frequently takes form around the acreage limitation. In
1902, in the Reclamation Act, Congress apparently intended to declare for a
wide sharing of the benefits from the use of national resources in the form of
land or funds. It said that irrigation water obtained through the use of
these funds should go only to 160 acres within one ownership. The
social ideal of the time was the family-owned and family-operated farm,
and it seemed that 160 acres of irrigated land, coupled perhaps with some
nonirrigated land, was enough for a respectable living in the American way
of the time.

Many of the owners of land in old irrigation districts that were developed before or independently of the Reclamation Act have overused their water supply. They now want federal loans and grants (reclamation works) to get more water on their land. Without the extra water, their land will lose great value. But they have established large properties, and they object to selling some of their land to veterans or to other newcomers who want to start in. They ask that the sharing provision be put aside. The more they have overused their water supply and let their properties run down, the more they need government funds and the less they are willing to accept one of the two conservation purposes of those funds. The reward for neglect is to be large.

Before the public are also the Army Engineers and the Bureau of Reclamation. The former, moving upstream into competition with the Bureau on King's River and elsewhere, are able—because of a legislative lag—to offer the large landowners water without the requirement that the old conservation idea of sharing benefits be observed. In order to stay active in that region the Bureau may yet be forced to rise above principle and find competitive ways of its own to undo the intent and action of Congress as expressed in the Reclamation Act.

This type of erosion of one of the two original conservation purposes of that act seems to be a matter of indifference to the administration and Congress. Yet once the breach in the basic act and purpose is made, at King's River or on the older developments, the whole process of obtaining a social gain from the use of public funds and other resources is soon flooded out. Much of the justification for the use of public resources goes downstream with it. The question is bound to be raised: Why devote public money in ways that will cause the growth of factory farms, as long as there are more socially valuable conservation purposes to be served elsewhere?

"UNFINISHED BUSINESS"

The unfinished conservation jobs pile up in numbers and in size if we are once convinced that growing population and increasing industrialization both at home and abroad and consequently an expanding demand, along with generally higher prices, are our lot for the next quarter- or half-century.

The articles in this issue of *The Annals* indicate a good number of those jobs. There is a high probability that we shall not be able to escape the stringencies involved and a consequent slowing-down of our rising standard of living without looking a little more closely at the end use of some of our natural resources. Conservation of materials for the essential needs may have to be obtained at the expense of the less essential parts of the economy. This is obviously the least desirable and most difficult way to conserve, but we may have to face up to it.

MINERALS

In minerals, for example, practically none of the long-term predictions that take account of foreign supply and demand as well as our own allow us to think of an adequate supply at the relatively low prices to which we were once accustomed. Is it unreasonable to think about channeling available supplies to those places where they will make the greatest contribution to our economic growth? Can the producers of nickel and chrome, for example, find some way of diverting those metals away from luxury display on automobiles to more vital parts of our industrial organization? The conservation gain could be considerable, and perhaps more than could be accomplished through more expensive forms of conservation in primary and secondary recovery.

In addition, is there not some better conservation and supply method than the one which we are applying to marginal mineral operations? Copper is one illustration. In an emergency we pay premium prices for the production of high-cost Michigan copper. Without them it could not be produced. When the apparent emergency is over, the mines are idled and flooded. Large loans plus premium prices plus years of manpower and delay are needed to get them into operation again. Surely this is not the best process that can be devised by the mind of man. With a more or less permanent world copper shortage for the rest of the century, there seems to be some room and place for discussing the possibility of a more continuous multiple-price system.

Since much of our future mineral procurement is going to be in foreign fields, it can pertinently be pointed out that the attempt to obtain scarce minerals by handling marginal producers abroad on the same short-term basis that we have used on the Michigan copper producers is bound to flare back on us. The attempt to squeeze the marginal Bolivian tin producers down to the Malayan cost and price level (although undertaken for the laudable purpose of preventing the Malayan producers from living luxuriously at our expense under a high Bolivian price-umbrella) has probably done a great deal of good to our Argentine rivals in Bolivia, and to no one else. This is on a par with our post-Korean tendency to rush out, wave a check, double prices, and expect new sources of minerals to be opened up the next day. It is also tied up with the interesting but controversial concept that the ultimate function of all the raw materials in the world is that of supporting the high American standard of living.

PETROLEUM

The need for some serious rethinking of our petroleum conservation is underlined by Mr. George Lamb's estimate . . . that there will be no petroleum at all available from any source for space heating or steam raising by 1975, and not quite enough to supply the demand for gasoline and motor oils by that time. With all allowance for necessarily wide ranges of error in any such estimate, and for past predictions of shortages that have not developed, this picture by a man who is perhaps the coal industry's leading economist should hardly be ignored. His estimate warrants all the study and revision the fuel industries can give it.

Implicit in his estimate is a change-over that may not only involve an investment within a short twenty-five years of enough resources to double the present coal production. It may affect also the values of all the residences, offices, and factories that would have to convert from oil or gas heat to electric heating. It may involve the values of continuing to equip new buildings and steam plants with oil or gas heat, as well as the value of new and old automobiles. It may finally, after the petroleum production peak has been passed, include one price race between gasoline and motor oil users (who cannot use coal) on the one hand, and the space-heating and steam-raising users (who can) on the other, and another price race between coal and petroleum in which the production costs of coal are not important.

If any such major transition is ahead of us, it seems impossible to escape the need, first, for pressing a series of conservation questions some time before that period begins. Are all the desirable conservation measures in oil production now being undertaken? To what extent do present prices and production quotas allow for really complete exhaustion of the fields without the necessity for closing down and waiting for higher prices before full secondary recovery can take place? What effect, if any, does the present tax privilege of the industry (the depletion allowance) have on conservation in the extraction process?

But here again it seems impossible to avoid the problem of end use. If, at some later time, the market is going to be called upon to create very high prices in order to achieve the objective of driving out most of the users of petroleum for space heating and steam raising, is it possible for the fuel industries to ease any such transition in advance, in ways that may be less costly to all groups of consumers than those involved in the double price race indicated, with all its probable wide repercussions on property values? And if that is not possible for them to do, how can it be done?

Incidentally, what such a change-over and such a price race in the United States might do to world petroleum prices, and through them to the European economy, is worth a second thought. As little as 40 million tons of coal has stood between western Europe and Communism several times since 1946. Several times Europe has been forced to devote a large share of the American aid to purchasing American coal at high delivered prices. It will probably, by 1975, have to depend for energy largely on Middle Eastern oil. A doubling or tripling of the world fuel price because of marginal American demands might have explosive results.

LUMBER AND PULP

The probability of increasing shortages and prices in the lumber and pulp industries brings us sharply back to the question of obtaining some real conservation through reforestation, better cutting, and less wasteful use; for the price of end-use conservation is a completely undesirable censorship. We may know and regret that high-priced pulp has had a part in forcing a number of independent newspapers out of business, and that a good many forests are used to produce some hundred million comic books. The permanent national economic gain from that, or even from using a good-sized forest each week to enable all our department stores to say in four pages what they used to say in a half-page, may also be questioned; but there seems to be nothing the nation can afford to do about it. The main task remains in the conservation and replacement of the growing stock, and that seems to be one of the most neglected of all.

LACK OF BASIC FACTS

A series of other questions might be pressed about our soil, range, water, and watershed conservation work, and many of them are suggested by the articles in this issue. What is really astonishing in all this land and water work is that the nation has as yet not established any preference and priority list for its conservation aid. Congress may grant $400 and loan $100 on an acre of reclamation land without ever having before it any comparisons which indicate whether the same or greater crop results or social benefits may not be obtained for much less money on some presently eroded or undrained lands. The cost-benefit ratios of the various conservation and development agencies are not comparable, and often do not give adequate basis for determining the conservation needs, let alone the reasonable contributions which the benefited communities may be expected to make to this work. A by-product of our neglect is that really depressed areas, such as some of those in the Rio Grande Basin, can never get enough help to get off the ground, overcome their conservation failures, and become prosperous and independent.

THE TASK AHEAD

Enough has probably been said here . . . to indicate that the conservation job is far from completed, but that, instead, a series of major problems and tasks stretch out before the people of the nation, and especially before the resource owners and the workers in their industries.

It will be noted that the problems spread across the resources. They also spread across the various specialized fields of study and the disciplines of the colleges and universities. Almost every one of them reaches across the curtains which committees of Congress and departments of the Executive Branch set about themselves, as well as across the borders of the professional societies. This fact may, in this specialized age, have something to do with our failure to grapple with them more thoroughly.

FINDINGS BY SPECIALISTS

Specialists can contribute a great deal. It would seem highly desirable, for example, that the distinguished deans of our colleges of forestry be asked to sit together and sift out the truth and the facts in the controversy about the extent of bad cutting of our forest resources, and in the even more important related controversy about the supply-demand-price situation that we may expect within the next generation or so in forest products. That would be a very considerable national service, and should be undertaken promptly, with resources adequate to cover the field. It is long overdue. The nation certainly has a right to know, beyond what may be the self-interested claims of government officials or of industries, what the situation really is.

But specialists, as they themselves will readily admit, are not enough to provide all the value judgments that the nation needs. The problems are complicated, and in the end the whole society has to decide the purposes for which natural resources are to be used, and the costs which it is willing to pay to achieve these purposes.

SYNTHESIS BY LEARNED AND PROFESSIONAL SOCIETIES

In the premises, which include the present atomization of the conservation groups, it would be exceedingly helpful if the learned and professional societies were to take on this task. They would, first of all, have to go pragmatically, resource by resource, into the question of whether there is a dichotomy between society and time on the one hand, and the immediate interests of the resource owner on the other. When there is a serious difference, they would have to see what social engineering could be developed to reconcile both private and public interests. For those purposes they would need to group some of their ablest and most disinterested people together for quite a while. They would need to draw heavily on the resource owners and workers for counsel, and on the experts for work. They would need to take into account the international role, whatever it is, that Congress and the administration want the nation to play, and the demands on our resources involved in it. They would have to do some very independent thinking of their own.

Their findings would, I believe, carry far more weight with everybody, from the smallest farmer to the oldest senator, than the studies and thinking of either industry or government bodies; for they would be dependent on, or beholden to, neither. If they did their work well, the economy and the people of the nation would be the great gainers.

When they were through, a somewhat more united and deeply rooted conservation movement might be able to grow up, and that, too, would be helpful to the nation.

six from silent spring

RACHEL CARSON

With Silent Spring *(1962), which first appeared serialized
in the magazine* The New Yorker, *Rachel Carson
(1907–1964) played a decisive role in awakening the
United States to the danger of pesticides (especially DDT)
to the natural environment. She had a graduate degree
from Johns Hopkins University and, in 1936, joined the
Department of the Interior's Bureau of Fisheries as a
working biologist. Between 1949 and 1952 she was editor
of the Fish and Wildlife Service and in 1951 published
the very popular book* The Sea Around Us. *Although
critics attacked her as naïve and simplistic, Rachel Carson's
professional training as a scientist stood her in good
stead and she was able to bring a unique combination
of expertise in biology and writing to the task of alerting
the nation to a major environmental catastrophe.*

As man proceeds toward his announced goal of the
conquest of nature, he has written a depressing record of
destruction, directed not only against the earth he inhabits
but against the life that shares it with him. The history
of the recent centuries has its black passages—the slaughter
of the buffalo on the western plains, the massacre of the
shorebirds by the market gunners, the near-extermination of
the egrets for their plumage. Now, to these and others
like them, we are adding a new chapter and a new kind of
havoc—the direct killing of birds, mammals, fishes, and
indeed practically every form of wildlife by chemical
insecticides indiscriminately sprayed on the land.

Source: Rachel Carson, *Silent Spring* (Cambridge, Mass.: Houghton
Mifflin, 1962), pp. 85–100. Copyright © 1962 by Rachel L.
Carson. Reprinted by permission of the publisher, Houghton
Mifflin Company.

Under the philosophy that now seems to guide our destinies, nothing must get in the way of the man with the spray gun. The incidental victims of his crusade against insects count as nothing; if robins, pheasants, raccoons, cats, or even livestock happen to inhabit the same bit of earth as the target insects and to be hit by the rain of insect-killing poisons no one must protest.

The citizen who wishes to make a fair judgment of the question of wildlife loss is today confronted with a dilemma. On the one hand conservationists and many wildlife biologists assert that the losses have been severe and in some cases even catastrophic. On the other hand the control agencies tend to deny flatly and categorically that such losses have occurred, or that they are of any importance if they have. Which view are we to accept?

The credibility of the witness is of first importance. The professional wildlife biologist on the scene is certainly best qualified to discover and interpret wildlife loss. The entomologist, whose specialty is insects, is not so qualified by training, and is not psychologically disposed to look for undesirable side effects of his control program. Yet it is the control men in state and federal governments—and of course the chemical manufacturers—who steadfastly deny the facts reported by the biologists and declare they see little evidence of harm to wildlife. Like the priest and the Levite in the biblical story, they choose to pass by on the other side and to see nothing. Even if we charitably explain their denials as due to the shortsightedness of the specialist and the man with an interest this does not mean we must accept them as qualified witnesses.

The best way to form our own judgment is to look at some of the major control programs and learn, from observers familiar with the ways of wildlife, and unbiased in favor of chemicals, just what has happened in the wake of a rain of poison falling from the skies into the world of wildlife.

To the bird watcher, the suburbanite who derives joy from birds in his garden, the hunter, the fisherman or the explorer of wild regions, anything that destroys the wildlife of an area for even a single year has deprived him of pleasure to which he has a legitimate right. This is a valid point of view. Even if, as has sometimes happened, some of the birds and mammals and fishes are able to re-establish themselves after a single spraying, a great and real harm has been done.

But such re-establishment is unlikely to happen. Spraying tends to be repetitive, and a single exposure from which the wildlife populations might have a chance to recover is a rarity. What usually results is a poisoned environment, a lethal trap in which not only the resident populations succumb but those who come in as migrants as well. The larger the area sprayed the more serious the harm, because no oases of safety remain. Now, in a decade marked by insect-control programs in which many thousands or even millions of acres are sprayed as a unit, a decade in which private and community spraying has also surged steadily upward, a record of destruction and death of American wildlife has accumulated. Let us look at some of these programs and see what has happened.

During the fall of 1959 some 27,000 acres in southeastern Michigan, including numerous suburbs of Detroit, were heavily dusted from the air with pellets of aldrin, one of the most dangerous of all the chlorinated hydrocarbons. The program was conducted by the Michigan Department of Agriculture with the cooperation of the United States Department of Agriculture; its announced purpose was control of the Japanese beetle.

Little need was shown for this drastic and dangerous action. On the contrary, Walter P. Nickell, one of the best-known and best-informed naturalists in the state, who spends much of his time in the field with long periods in southern Michigan every summer, declared: "For more than thirty years, to my direct knowledge, the Japanese beetle has been present in the city of Detroit in small numbers. The numbers have not shown any appreciable increase in all this lapse of years. I have yet to see a single Japanese beetle [in 1959] other than the few caught in Government catch traps in Detroit . . . Everything is being kept so secret that I have not yet been able to obtain any information whatsoever to the effect that they have increased in numbers."

An official release by the state agency merely declared that the beetle had "put in its appearance" in the areas designated for the aerial attack upon it. Despite the lack of justification the program was launched, with the state providing the manpower and supervising the operation, the federal government providing equipment and additional men, and the communities paying for the insecticide.

The Japanese beetle, an insect accidentally imported into the United States, was discovered in New Jersey in 1916, when a few shiny beetles of a metallic green color were seen in a nursery near Riverton. The beetles, at first unrecognized, were finally identified as a common inhabitant of the main islands of Japan. Apparently they had entered the United States on nursery stock imported before restrictions were established in 1912.

From its original point of entrance the Japanese beetle has spread rather widely throughout many of the states east of the Mississippi, where conditions of temperature and rainfall are suitable for it. Each year some outward movement beyond the existing boundaries of its distribution usually takes place. In the eastern areas where the beetles have been longest established, attempts have been made to set up natural controls. Where this has been done, the beetle populations have been kept at relatively low levels, as many records attest.

Despite the record of reasonable control in eastern areas, the midwestern states now on the fringe of the beetle's range have launched an attack worthy of the most deadly enemy instead of only a moderately destructive insect, employing the most dangerous chemicals distributed in a manner that exposes large numbers of people, their domestic animals, and all wildlife to the poison intended for the beetle. As a result these Japanese beetle programs have caused shocking destruction of animal life and have exposed human beings to undeniable hazard. Sections of Michigan, Kentucky, Iowa, Indiana, Illinois, and Missouri are all experiencing a rain of chemicals in the name of beetle control.

The Michigan spraying was one of the first large-scale attacks on the Japanese beetle from the air. The choice of aldrin, one of the deadliest of all chemicals, was not determined by any peculiar suitability for Japanese beetle control, but simply by the wish to save money—aldrin was the cheapest of the compounds available. While the state in its official release to the press acknowledged that aldrin is a "poison," it implied that no harm could come to human beings in the heavily populated areas to which the chemical was applied. (The official answer to the query "What precautions should I take?" was "For you, none.") An official of the Federal Aviation Agency was later quoted in the local press to the effect that "this is a safe operation" and a representative of the Detroit Department of Parks and Recreation added his assurance that "the dust is harmless to humans and will not hurt plants or pets." One must assume that none of these officials had consulted the published and readily available reports of the United States Public Health Service, the Fish and Wildlife Service, and other evidence of the extremely poisonous nature of aldrin.

Acting under the Michigan pest control law which allows the state to spray indiscriminately without notifying or gaining permission of individual landowners, the low-lying planes began to fly over the Detroit area. The city authorities and the Federal Aviation Agency were immediately besieged by calls from worried citizens. After receiving nearly 800 calls in a single hour, the police begged radio and television stations and newspapers to "tell the watchers what they were seeing and advise them it was safe," according to the Detroit *News.* The Federal Aviation Agency's safety officer assured the public that "the planes are carefully supervised" and "are authorized to fly low." In a somewhat mistaken attempt to allay fears, he added that the planes had emergency valves that would allow them to dump their entire load instantaneously. This, fortunately, was not done, but as the planes went about their work the pellets of insecticide fell on beetles and humans alike, showers of "harmless" poison descending on people shopping or going to work and on children out from school for the lunch hour. Housewives swept the granules from porches and sidewalks, where they are said to have "looked like snow." As pointed out later by the Michigan Audubon Society, "In the spaces between shingles on roofs, in eaves-troughs, in the cracks in bark and twigs, the little white pellets of aldrin-and-clay, no bigger than a pin head, were lodged by the millions . . . When the snow and rain came, every puddle became a possible death potion."

Within a few days after the dusting operation, the Detroit Audubon Society began receiving calls about the birds. According to the Society's secretary, Mrs. Ann Boyes, "The first indication that the people were concerned about the spray was a call I received on Sunday morning from a woman who reported that coming home from church she saw an alarming number of dead and dying birds. The spraying there had been done on Thursday. She said there were no birds at all flying in the area, that she had found at least a dozen [dead] in her backyard and that the neighbors had found dead squirrels." All other calls received by Mrs. Boyes that day reported "a great many dead birds and no live ones . . . People who had maintained bird feeders said there were no birds at all at their feeders." Birds picked up in a dying condition showed the typical symptoms of insecticide poisoning—tremoring, loss of ability to fly, paralysis, convulsions.

Nor were birds the only forms of life immediately affected. A local veterinarian reported that his office was full of clients with dogs and cats that had suddenly sickened. Cats, who so meticulously groom their coats and lick their paws, seemed to be most affected. Their illness took the form of severe diarrhea, vomiting, and convulsions. The only advice the veterinarian could give his clients was not to let the animals out unnecessarily, or to wash the paws promptly if they did so. (But the chlorinated hydrocarbons cannot be washed even from fruits or vegetables, so little protection could be expected from this measure.)

Despite the insistence of the City-County Health Commissioner that the birds must have been killed by "some other kind of spraying" and that the outbreak of throat and chest irritations that followed the exposure to aldrin must have been due to "something else," the local Health Department received a constant stream of complaints. A prominent Detroit internist was called upon to treat four of his patients within an hour after they had been exposed while watching the planes at work. All had similar symptoms: nausea, vomiting, chills, fever, extreme fatigue, and coughing.

The Detroit experience has been repeated in many other communities as pressure has mounted to combat the Japanese beetle with chemicals. At Blue Island, Illinois, hundreds of dead and dying birds were picked up. Data collected by birdbanders here suggest that 80 per cent of the songbirds were sacrificed. In Joliet, Illinois, some 3000 acres were treated with heptachlor in 1959. According to reports from a local sportsmen's club, the bird population within the treated area was "virtually wiped out." Dead rabbits, muskrats, opossums, and fish were also found in numbers, and one of the local schools made the collection of insecticide-poisoned birds a science project.

Perhaps no community has suffered more for the sake of a beetleless world than Sheldon, in eastern Illinois, and adjacent areas in Iroquois County. In 1954 the United States Department of Agriculture and the Illinois Agriculture Department began a program to eradicate the Japanese beetle along the line of its advance into Illinois, holding out the hope, and indeed the assurance, that intensive spraying would destroy the populations of the invading insect. The first "eradication" took place that year, when dieldrin was applied to 1400 acres by air. Another 2600 acres were treated similarly in 1955, and the task was presumably considered complete. But more and more chemical treatments were called for, and by the end of 1961 some 131,000 acres had been covered. Even in the first years of the program it was apparent that heavy losses were occurring among wildlife and domestic animals. The chemical treatments were continued, nevertheless, without consultation with either the United States Fish and Wildlife Service or the Illinois Game Management Division. (In the spring of 1960, however, officials of the federal Department of Agriculture appeared before a congressional committee in opposition to a bill that would require just such prior consultation. They declared blandly that the bill was unnecessary because cooperation and consultation were "usual." These officials were quite unable to recall situations where cooperation had not taken place "at the Washington level." In the same hearings they stated clearly their unwillingness to consult with state fish and game departments.)

Although funds for chemical control came in never-ending streams, the biologists of the Illinois Natural History Survey who attempted to measure the damage to wildlife had to operate on a financial shoestring. A mere $1100 was available for the employment of a field assistant in 1954 and no special funds were provided in 1955. Despite these crippling difficulties, the biologists assembled facts that collectively paint a picture of almost unparalleled wildlife destruction—destruction that became obvious as soon as the program got under way.

Conditions were made to order for poisoning insect-eating birds, both in the poisons used and in the events set in motion by their application. In the early programs at Sheldon, dieldrin was applied at the rate of 3 pounds to the acre. To understand its effect on birds one need only remember that in laboratory experiments on quail dieldrin has proved to be about 50 times as poisonous as DDT. The poison spread over the landscape at Sheldon was therefore roughly equivalent to 150 pounds of DDT per acre! And this was a minimum, because there seems to have been some overlapping of treatments along field borders and in corners.

As the chemical penetrated the soil the poisoned beetle grubs crawled out on the surface of the ground, where they remained for some time before they died, attractive to insect-eating birds. Dead and dying insects of various species were conspicuous for about two weeks after the treatment. The effect on the bird populations could easily have been foretold. Brown thrashers, starlings, meadowlarks, grackles, and pheasants were virtually wiped out. Robins were "almost annihilated," according to the biologists' report. Dead earthworms had been seen in numbers after a gentle rain; probably the robins had fed on the poisoned worms. For other birds, too, the once beneficial rain had been changed, through the evil power of the poison introduced into their world, into an agent of destruction. Birds seen drinking and bathing in puddles left by rain a few days after the spraying were inevitably doomed.

The birds that survived may have been rendered sterile. Although a few nests were found in the treated area, a few with eggs, none contained young birds.

Among the mammals ground squirrels were virtually annihilated; their bodies were found in attitudes characteristic of violent death by poisoning. Dead muskrats were found in the treated areas, dead rabbits in the fields. The fox squirrel had been a relatively common animal in the town; after the spraying it was gone.

It was a rare farm in the Sheldon area that was blessed by the presence of a cat after the war on beetles was begun. Ninety per cent of all the farm cats fell victims to the dieldrin during the first season of spraying. This might have been predicted because of the black record of these poisons in other places. Cats are extremely sensitive to all insecticides and especially so, it seems, to dieldrin. In western Java in the course of the antimalarial program carried out by the World Health Organization, many cats are reported to have died. In central Java so many were killed that the price of a cat more than doubled. Similarly, the World Health Organization, spraying in Venezuela, is reported to have reduced cats to the status of a rare animal.

In Sheldon it was not only the wild creatures and the domestic companions that were sacrificed in the campaign against an insect. Observations on several flocks of sheep and a herd of beef cattle are indicative of the poisoning and death

that threatened livestock as well. The Natural History Survey report describes
one of these episodes as follows:

> *The sheep ... were driven into a small, untreated blue-grass pasture*
> *across a gravel road from a field which had been treated with dieldrin*
> *spray on May 6. Evidently some spray had drifted across the road into*
> *the pasture, for the sheep began to show symptoms of intoxication*
> *almost at once ... They lost interest in food and displayed extreme*
> *restlessness, following the pasture fence around and around apparently*
> *searching for a way out ... [They] refused to be driven, bleated almost*
> *continuously, and stood with their heads lowered; they were finally*
> *carried from the pasture ... They displayed great desire for water. Two*
> *of the sheep were found dead in the stream passing through the pasture,*
> *and the remaining sheep were repeatedly driven out of the stream,*
> *several having to be dragged forcibly from the water. Three of the*
> *sheep eventually died; those remaining recovered to all outward*
> *appearances.*

This, then, was the picture at the end of 1955. Although the chemical war
went on in succeeding years, the trickle of research funds dried up completely.
Requests for money for wildlife-insecticide research were included in
annual budgets submitted to the Illinois legislature by the Natural History
Survey, but were invariably among the first items to be eliminated. It was not
until 1960 that money was somehow found to pay the expenses of one field
assistant—to do work that could easily have occupied the time of four men.

The desolate picture of wildlife loss had changed little when the biologists
resumed the studies broken off in 1955. In the meantime, the chemical had been
changed to the even more toxic aldrin, *100 to 300 times* as toxic as DDT in
tests on quail. By 1960, every species of wild mammal known to inhabit the
area had suffered losses. It was even worse with the birds. In the small town of
Donovan the robins had been wiped out, as had the grackles, starlings, and
brown thrashers. These and many other birds were sharply reduced elsewhere.
Pheasant hunters felt the effects of the beetle campaign sharply. The number of
broods produced on treated lands fell off by some 50 per cent, and the number of
young in a brood declined. Pheasant hunting, which had been good in these
areas in former years, was virtually abandoned as unrewarding.

In spite of the enormous havoc that had been wrought in the name of
eradicating the Japanese beetle, the treatment of more than 100,000 acres in
Iroquois County over an eight-year period seems to have resulted in only
temporary suppression of the insect, which continues its westward movement.
The full extent of the toll that has been taken by this largely ineffective program
may never be known, for the results measured by the Illinois biologists are a
minimum figure. If the research program had been adequately financed to
permit full coverage, the destruction revealed would have been even more
appalling. But in the eight years of the program, only about $6000 was provided
for biological field studies. Meanwhile the federal government had spent about
$375,000 for control work and additional thousands had been provided by the

state. The amount spent for research was therefore a small fraction of 1 per cent of the outlay for the chemical program.

These midwestern programs have been conducted in a spirit of crisis, as though the advance of the beetle presented an extreme peril justifying any means to combat it. This of course is a distortion of the facts, and if the communities that have endured these chemical drenchings had been familiar with the earlier history of the Japanese beetle in the United States they would surely have been less acquiescent.

The eastern states, which had the good fortune to sustain their beetle invasion in the days before the synthetic insecticides had been invented, have not only survived the invasion but have brought the insect under control by means that represented no threat whatever to other forms of life. There has been nothing comparable to the Detroit or Sheldon sprayings in the East. The effective methods there involved the bringing into play of natural forces of control which have the multiple advantages of permanence and environmental safety.

During the first dozen years after its entry into the United States, the beetle increased rapidly, free of the restraints that in its native land hold it in check. But by 1945 it had become a pest of only minor importance throughout much of the territory over which it had spread. Its decline was largely a consequence of the importation of parasitic insects from the Far East and of the establishment of disease organisms fatal to it.

Between 1920 and 1933, as a result of diligent searching throughout the native range of the beetle, some 34 species of predatory or parasitic insects had been imported from the Orient in an effort to establish natural control. Of these, five became well established in the eastern United States. The most effective and widely distributed is a parasitic wasp from Korea and China, *Tiphia vernalis*. The female *Tiphia*, finding a beetle grub in the soil, injects a paralyzing fluid and attaches a single egg to the undersurface of the grub. The young wasp, hatching as a larva, feeds on the paralyzed grub and destroys it. In some 25 years, colonies of *Tiphia* were introduced into 14 eastern states in a cooperative program of state and federal agencies. The wasp became widely established in this area and is generally credited by entomologists with an important role in bringing the beetle under control.

An even more important role has been played by a bacterial disease that affects beetles of the family to which the Japanese beetle belongs—the scarabaeids. It is a highly specific organism, attacking no other type of insects, harmless to earthworms, warm-blooded animals, and plants. The spores of the disease occur in soil. When ingested by a foraging beetle grub they multiply prodigiously in its blood, causing it to turn an abnormally white color, hence the popular name, "milky disease."

Milky disease was discovered in New Jersey in 1933. By 1938 it was rather widely prevalent in the older areas of Japanese beetle infestation. In 1939 a control program was launched, directed at speeding up the spread of the disease. No method had been developed for growing the disease organism in an artificial medium, but a satisfactory substitute was evolved; infected grubs are ground up, dried, and combined with chalk. In the standard mixture a gram of dust contains 100 million spores. Between 1939 and 1953 some 94,000 acres in 14 eastern states were treated in a cooperative federal-state program; other areas on federal lands were treated; and an unknown but extensive area was treated by private organizations or individuals. By 1945, milky spore disease was raging among the beetle populations of Connecticut, New York, New Jersey, Delaware, and Maryland. In some test areas infection of grubs had reached as high as 94 per cent. The distribution program was discontinued as a governmental enterprise in 1953 and production was taken over by a private laboratory, which continues to supply individuals, garden clubs, citizens' associations, and all others interested in beetle control.

The eastern areas where this program was carried out now enjoy a high degree of natural protection from the beetle. The organism remains viable in the soil for years and therefore becomes to all intents and purposes permanently established, increasing in effectiveness, and being continuously spread by natural agencies.

Why, then, with this impressive record in the East, were the same procedures not tried in Illinois and the other midwestern states where the chemical battle of the beetles is now being waged with such fury?

We are told that inoculation with milky spore disease is "too expensive"— although no one found it so in the 14 eastern states in the 1940's. And by what sort of accounting was the "too expensive" judgment reached? Certainly not by any that assessed the true costs of the total destruction wrought by such programs as the Sheldon spraying. This judgment also ignores the fact that inoculation with the spores need be done only once; the first cost is the only cost.

We are told also that milky spore disease cannot be used on the periphery of the beetle's range because it can be established only where a large grub population is *already* present in the soil. Like many other statements in support of spraying, this one needs to be questioned. The bacterium that causes milky spore disease has been found to infect at least 40 other species of beetles which collectively have quite a wide distribution and would in all probability serve to establish the disease even where the Japanese beetle population is very small or nonexistent. Furthermore, because of the long viability of the spores in soil they can be introduced even in the complete absence of grubs, as on the fringe of the present beetle infestation, there to await the advancing population.

Those who want immediate results, at whatever cost, will doubtless continue to use chemicals against the beetle. So will those who favor the modern trend to built-in obsolescence, for chemical control is self-perpetuating, needing frequent and costly repetition.

On the other hand, those who are willing to wait an extra season or two for full results will turn to milky disease; they will be rewarded with lasting control that becomes more, rather than less effective with the passage of time.

An extensive program of research is under way in the United States Department of Agriculture laboratory at Peoria, Illinois, to find a way to culture the organism of milky disease on an artificial medium. This will greatly reduce its cost and should encourage its more extensive use. After years of work, some success has now been reported. When this "breakthrough" is thoroughly established perhaps some sanity and perspective will be restored to our dealings with the Japanese beetle, which at the peak of its depredations never justified the nightmare excesses of some of these midwestern programs.

Incidents like the eastern Illinois spraying raise a question that is not only scientific but moral. The question is whether any civilization can wage relentless war on life without destroying itself, and without losing the right to be called civilized.

These insecticides are not selective poisons; they do not single out the one species of which we desire to be rid. Each of them is used for the simple reason that it is a deadly poison. It therefore poisons all life with which it comes in contact: the cat beloved of some family, the farmer's cattle, the rabbit in the field, and the horned lark out of the sky. These creatures are innocent of any harm to man. Indeed, by their very existence they and their fellows make his life more pleasant. Yet he rewards them with a death that is not only sudden but horrible. Scientific observers at Sheldon described the symptoms of a meadowlark found near death: "Although it lacked muscular coordination and could not fly or stand, it continued to beat its wings and clutch with its toes while lying on its side. Its beak was held open and breathing was labored." Even more pitiful was the mute testimony of the dead ground squirrels, which "exhibited a characteristic attitude in death. The back was bowed, and the forelegs with the toes of the feet tightly clenched were drawn close to the thorax . . . The head and neck were outstretched and the mouth often contained dirt, suggesting that the dying animal had been biting at the ground."

By acquiescing in an act that can cause such suffering to a living creature, who among us is not diminished as a human being?

seven
can we survive?

BARRY COMMONER

*Barry Commoner (b. 1917) earned his Ph.D. at Harvard
University and has taught at Washington University in
St. Louis since 1947. As a specialist in virus biosynthesis
and the chemical basis of inheritance, Dr. Commoner
became concerned about the effects of nuclear weapons
testing in the 1950s and was one of the leaders in
mobilizing scientific opinion for demand of a ban on such
testing. His concern for radiation pollution broadened,
and today he is one of the leading spokesmen for socially
responsible science. He is the director of the Center
for the Biology of Natural Systems at Washington
University, and author of* Science and Survival *(1966).*

No one can escape the enormous fact that California has
changed. What was once desert has become the most
productive land in the world. The once lonely mountain
tops are crisscrossed with humming power lines.
Powerful industries, from old ones like steel to the most
modern aerospace and electronic operations, have been built.
California has become one of the most fruitful, one of the
richest places on the surface of the earth. This is all
change, and it is good.

But there are other changes in California. Its vigorous
growth has been achieved by many men and women
who came to give their children a healthy place to live.
Now, however, when school children in Los Angeles run
out to the playing fields, they are confronted by the
warning: "Do not exercise strenuously or breathe too
deeply during heavy smog conditions." For the sunshine
that once bathed the land in golden light has been
blotted out by deadly smog. In a number of California
towns the water supplies now contain levels of nitrate above

Source: Barry Commoner, "Can We Survive?" *Washington
Monthly* 1 (December 1969): 12–21. Reprinted by permission
of the author and the publisher.

the limit recommended by the U.S. Public Health Service; given to infants, nitrate can cause a fatal disorder, methemoglobinemia, and pediatricians have recommended the use of bottled water for infant formulas. The natural resources of California, once a magnet that attracted thousands who sought a good life, now harbor threats to health. Beaches that once sparkled in the sun are polluted with oil and foul-smelling deposits. Rivers that once teemed with fish run sluggishly to the sea. The once famous crabs in San Francisco Bay are dying. Redwoods are toppling from the banks of eroding streams. All this, too, is change, and it is bad.

Thus, much of the good that has been produced in California, through the intelligence and hard work of its people, has been won at a terrible cost. That cost is the possible destruction of the very capital which has been invested to create the wealth of the state—its environment.

The environment makes up a huge, enormously complex living machine—an ecosystem—and every human activity depends on the integrity and proper functioning of that machine. Without the ecosystem's green plants, there would be no oxygen for smelters and furnaces, let alone to support human and animal life. Without the action of plants and animals in aquatic systems, there would be no pure water to supply agriculture, industry, and the cities. Without the biological processes that have gone on in the soil for thousands of years, there would be neither food crops, oil, nor coal. This machine is our biological capital, the basic apparatus on which our total productivity depends. If it is destroyed, agriculture and industry will come to naught; yet the greatest threats to the environmental system are due to agricultural and industrial activities. If the ecosystem is destroyed, man will go down with it; yet it is man who is destroying it. For in the eager search for the benefits of modern science and technology, we have become enticed into a nearly fatal illusion: that we have at last escaped from the dependence of man on the rest of nature. The truth is tragically different. We have become not less dependent on the balance of nature, but more dependent on it. Modern technology has so stressed the web of processes in the living environment at its most vulnerable points that there is little leeway left in the system. We are approaching the point of no return; our survival is at stake.

These are grim, alarming conclusions; but they are forced on us, I am convinced, by the evidence. Let us look at some of that evidence.

A good place to begin is the farm—on which so much of California's prosperity is based. The wealth created by agriculture is derived from the soil. In it we grow crops which convert inorganic materials—nitrogen, phosphorus, carbon, oxygen, and the other elements required by life—into organic materials —proteins, carbohydrates, fats, and vitamins—which comprise our food.

The soil, the plants that grow in it, the livestock raised on the land, and we ourselves are parts of a huge web of natural processes—endless, self-perpetuating cycles. Consider, for example, the behavior of nitrogen, an element of enormous nutritional importance, forming as it does the basis of proteins and other vital life substances. Most of the earth's available nitrogen is in the air, as nitrogen gas. This can enter the soil through nitrogen fixation, a process carried out by various bacteria, some of them living free in the soil and others associated with the roots of legumes such as clover. In nature, nitrogen also enters the soil from the wastes produced by animals. In both cases the nitrogen becomes incorporated into a complex organic material in the soil—humus. The humus slowly releases nitrogen through the action of soil microorganisms which finally convert it into nitrate. In turn, the nitrate is taken up by the roots of plants and is made into protein and other vital parts of the crop. In a natural situation the plant becomes food for animals, their wastes are returned to the soil, and the cycle is complete.

This cycle is an example of the biological capital that sustains us. How has this capital been used in California?

The huge success of agriculture in California is a matter of record; it forms the largest single element in the state's economy. To achieve this wealth a vast area in the center of the state has been transformed from a bare desert into the richest agricultural land in the nation. How has this been done? How has this transformation affected the continued usefulness of the soil system, especially the nitrogen cycle?

When the first farmers came to the San Joaquin Valley, they found fertile soil and sunshine; only water was needed to make the valley bloom. This was obtained first from local streams and later, increasingly, from wells which tapped the huge store of water that lay beneath the entire Central Valley. As the bountiful crops were taken, the soil, originally rich in nitrogen, became impoverished. To sustain crop productivity, inorganic nitrogen fertilizers were added to the soil. But with the loss of natural soil nitrogen, humus was depleted; as a result the soil became less porous, and less oxygen reached the roots, which were then less efficient in taking up the needed nutrients from the soil. The answer: more nitrogen fertilizer, for even if a smaller proportion is taken up by the crop, this can be overcome by using more fertilizer to begin with. California now uses more nitrogen fertilizer than any other state—an average of about 450 pounds per acre in 1959.

One of the rules of environmental biology is: "Everything has to go somewhere," and we may ask: Where did the extra nitrate added to the soil, but not taken up by the crops, go? The answer is clear: The unused nitrate was carried down into the soil, accumulating at greater and greater depths as the water table fell due to the continual pumping of irrigation water.

With the water table falling, agriculture in the Central Valley was headed for disaster; recognizing this fact, the state constructed the Friant-Kern Canal, which began to supply the valley with above-ground irrigation water beginning in 1951. Irrigation water must always be supplied to soil in amounts greater than that which is lost by evaporation; otherwise salts accumulate in the soil and the plants are killed. So, following the opening of the new canal, the valley water table began to rise toward its original level—carrying with it the long-accumulated nitrates in the soil.

Now there is another simple rule of environmental biology that is appropriate here: "Everything is connected to everything else." The valley towns soon learned this truth, as their drinking water supplies—which were taken from wells that tapped the rising level of underground water—began to show increasing concentrations of nitrate. In the 1950's, the Bureau of Sanitary

Engineering of the California Department of Public Health began to analyze
the nitrate content of city water supplies in the area. They had good reason for
this action, for in July, 1950, an article in the *Journal of the American
Water Works Association* had described 139 cases of infant methemoglobenemia
in the United States identified since 1947; 14 cases were fatal; all were attributed
to farm well water contaminated with more than 45 ppm of nitrate.

At first, only a few scattered instances of high nitrate levels were found in
valley water supplies. However, a study of 800 wells in southern California
counties in 1960 showed that 88 of them exceeded the 45 ppm limit; 188
wells had reached half that level. In that year, the U.S. Public Health Service
recommended that a nitrate level of 45 ppm should not be exceeded, warning:

> *Cases of infantile nitrate poisoning have been reported to arise
> from concentrations ranging from 66 to 1100 ppm. . . . Nitrate
> poisoning appears to be confined to infants during their first few months
> of life; adults drinking the same water are not affected, but breast-fed
> infants of mothers drinking such water may be poisoned. Cows
> drinking water containing nitrate may produce milk sufficiently high
> in nitrate to result in infant poisoning.*

In Delano, a 1952 analysis showed only traces of nitrate in the city water
supply; in 1966, analyses of three town wells obtained by the Delano Junior
Chamber of Commerce showed nitrate levels of 70–78 ppm. In 1968, a study by
the Water Resources Board, made in reply to a request by State Senator
Walter W. Stiern, showed:

> *Nitrate concentrations in groundwater underlying the vicinity of
> Delano are currently in excess of the limit . . . recommended by the
> U.S. Public Health Service . . . similar geologic and hydrologic
> conditions occur in other areas of the San Joaquin Valley and the state
> generally.*

So agricultural wealth of the Central Valley has been gained, but at a cost
that does not appear in the farmers' balance sheets—the general pollution of the
state's huge underground water reserves with nitrate. Fortunately, there
appear to be no reports of widespread acute infant methemoglobinemia in the
area as yet. However, the effects of chronic exposure to nitrates are poorly
understood. We do know that in animals nitrate may interfere with thyroid
metabolism, reduce the availability of vitamin A, and cause abortions.
Moreover, there is evidence that even small reductions in the oxygen available
to a developing human fetus—which might occur when the mother is exposed to
subcritical levels of nitrate—result in permanent damage to the brain. In sum,
the success of agriculture in the Central Valley has been won at a cost
which risks the health of the people.

Nor does the nitrogen problem end there. Much of the nitrogen fertilizer
applied to the soil of the Central Valley finds its way into the San Joaquin River,
which drains the irrigated fields. As a result, the river carries a huge load

of nitrate into the San Francisco Bay-Delta area. Here the added nitrate intrudes on another environmental cycle—the self-purifying biological processes of natural waters—bringing in its wake a new round of environmental destruction. The excess nitrate—along with excess phosphate from agricultural drainage and municipal wastes—stimulates the growth of algae in the waters of the Bay, causing the massive green scums that have become so common in the area. Such heavy overgrowths of algae soon die off, releasing organic matter which overwhelms the biological purification processes that normally remove it. As a result, the natural balance is destroyed; the water loses its oxygen; fish die; the water becomes foul with putrefying material. In the cooler words of the Department of Interior report on the San Joaquin Master Drain, "Problems resulting from nutrient enrichment and associated periodic dissolved oxygen depression are numerous in the Bay-Delta area."

So the agricultural practices of the great Central Valley have overwhelmed the natural nitrogen cycle of the soil with massive amounts of fertilizer; once this cycle was broken, the rivers were contaminated with nitrate. Reaching the Bay-Delta area, the excess nitrate has destroyed the natural balance of the self-purifying processes in these waters, with the foul results that are only too well known to those who live in that once-sparkling natural area.

This much is known fact. But once the natural cycles of the Bay-Delta waters are disrupted, other biological disasters may soon follow. At the present time, in a number of regions of the Bay-Delta waters, the bacterial count exceeds the limit recommended by the California Department of Public Health for water contact sports. This may be due to the entry of too much untreated sewage. But experience with the waters of New York harbor suggests another, more ominous, possibility which connects this problem, too, to the drainage of nutrients from agricultural areas, as well as from treated sewage. In New York harbor, in the period 1948–1968, there has been a 10–20-fold increase in the bacterial count despite a marked *improvement* in the sewage treatment facilities that drain into the bay. Here too there has been an increase in nitrate and phosphate nutrients, in this case largely from treated sewage effluent. The possibility exists that bacteria, entering the water from sewage or the soil, are now able to *grow* in the enriched waters of the bay. If this should prove to be the case, changes in water quality such as those which have occurred in the Bay-Delta area may lead to new, quite unexpected, health hazards. The soil contains many microorganisms which cause disease in human beings when they are first allowed to grow in a nutrient medium. There is a danger, then, that as the Bay-Delta waters become laden with organic matter released by dying algae (resulting from overgrowths stimulated by agricultural and municipal wastes), disease-producing microorganisms may find conditions suitable for growth, resulting in outbreaks of hitherto unknown types of water-borne disease.

Nor does the nitrogen story quite end here. We now know that a good deal of the excess nitrogen added to the soil by intensive fertilization practices may be released to the air in the form of ammonia or nitrogen oxides. In the air, these materials are gradually converted to nitrate and carried back to the ground by rain. In 1957, a national study of the nitrate content of rainfall showed excessively high levels in three heavily fertilized regions: the Corn Belt, Texas, and the Central Valley of California. There is increasing evidence that nitrate dissolved in rain can carry enough nutrient into even remote mountain lakes to cause algal overgrowths and so pollute waters still largely free of the effects of human wastes. Recent pollution problems in Lake Tahoe may originate in this way.

I cite these details in order to make clear a profound and inescapable fact of life: that the environment is a vast system of interlocking connections—among the soil, the water, the air, plants, animals, and ourselves—which forms an endless, dynamically interacting web. This network is the product of millions of years of evolution; each of its connections has been tested against the trial of time to achieve a balance which is stable and long-lasting. But the balance, the fine fabric of physical, chemical, and biological interconnections in the environment, is a delicate one; it hangs together only as a whole. Tear into it in one place—such as the soil of the Central Valley—and the fabric begins to unravel, spreading chaos from the soil to the rivers, to the Bay, to remote mountain lakes, to the mother and her infant child. The great Central Valley has become rich with the fruits of the land, but at a cost which has already been felt across the breadth of the state and which is yet to be fully paid.

Nor do we yet know how the destructive process can be halted, or if indeed it can be. In Lake Erie, where the natural balance of the water system has already been largely overwhelmed by excessive nutrients, no one has yet been able to devise a scheme to restore its original condition. The Bay-Delta waters may suffer the same fate. The recently released Kaiser Engineers' report on the San Francisco Bay-Delta Water Quality Control Program predicts that the drainage of agricultural nutrients (nitrogen and phosphorus) from the San Joaquin will continue unabated for at least the next 50 years if present agricultural practices persist. The report proposes a system which, to control only the deleterious effects of the drainage in the Bay-Delta area, will cost about $5 billion in that period. And even at that cost the plan will only transfer the problem to the ocean—where the waste nutrients are to be discharged—which can only bring disaster to this last remaining natural resource, on which so many of our future hopes must rest.

The root of the problem remains in the soil, for if the disrupted balance is not restored there, its destructive effects will only spread into further reaches of the environment. Tragically, each year of continued over-fertilization of the soil may make recovery increasingly difficult. For example, we know that inorganic nitrogen nutrients stop the nitrogen-fixing activity of microorganisms and may eventually kill them off or at least encourage them to mutate into non-fixing forms. If the natural fertility of the soil is ever to be restored, we may have to rely heavily on these microbial agents; but this becomes less and less possible as we continue to use massive amounts of fertilizer. In effect, like a drug addict, we may become "hooked" on continued heavy nitrogen fertilization and so become inescapably locked into a self-destructive course.

This same tragic tale of environmental disaster can be told of another prominent feature of California agriculture—insecticides. One important aspect of the biological capital on which agricultural productivity depends is the network of ecological relationships that relate insect pests to the plants on which they feed, and to the other insects that, in turn, prey on the pests. These natural relations serve to keep pest populations in check. Pests which require a particular plant as food are kept in check by their inability to spread onto other plants; the other insects which parasitize and prey upon them exert important biological control over the pest population.

What has happened in attempts to control cotton pests—where the great bulk of synthetic insecticide is used in the United States—shows how we have destroyed these natural relations and have allowed the natural pest-regulating machinery to break down. The massive use of the new insecticides has controlled some of the pests that once attacked cotton. But now the cotton plants are being attacked instead by new insects that were never previously known as pests of cotton. Moreover, the new pests are becoming increasingly resistant to insecticide, through the natural biological process of selection, in the course of inheritance, of resistant types. In Texas cotton fields, for example, in 1963 it took 50 times as much DDT to control insect pests as it did in 1961. The tobacco budworm, which now attacks cotton, has been found to be nearly immune to methylparathion, the most powerful of the widely used modern insecticides.

California, too, has begun to experience environmental disaster from the intensive use of insecticides. Consider only a single recent example. In 1965 the rich cotton fields of the Imperial Valley were invaded by the Pink Bollworm from Arizona. The Department of Agriculture began an "eradication" program based on a fixed schedule of repeated, heavy, insecticide sprays. The Pink Bollworm was controlled (but by no means "eradicated"); however, the cotton plants were then attacked by other insects which had previously caused no appreciable damage—the beet army worm and the cotton leaf perforator. The insecticide had killed off insects that were natural enemies of the army worms and perforators, which had in the meantime become resistant to the sprays. Catastrophic losses resulted. The problem is now so serious that Imperial Valley farmers have proposed the elimination of cotton plantings for a year in order to kill off the new pests, which cannot survive a year without food.

California is beginning to experience the kind of insecticide-induced disaster already common in Latin American experience. In the Cañete Valley of Peru, for example, DDT was used for the first time in 1949 to control cotton pests. Yields increased—temporarily. For soon the number of insects attacking the cotton grew from 7 to 13 and several of them had become resistant to the insecticides. By 1965, the cotton yields had dropped to half their previous value, and despite 15–25 insecticide applications, pest control was impossible. Productivity was restored only when massive insecticide application was halted and biological control was reestablished by importing insects to attack the pests.

These instances are, again, a warning that present agricultural practices may be destroying the biological capital which is essential to agricultural productivity —in this case, the natural population of insects that attack insect pests and keep them under the control of a natural balance. Again, if the ecologically

blind practice of massive insecticide treatment is allowed to continue, there is a
danger of permanently losing the natural protective insects—and agriculture
may become "hooked" on insecticides.

And here too we see disaster spreading through the environmental network.
In 1969, the Food and Drug Administration seized two shipments of canned
jack mackerel, an ocean fish originating from Terminal Island, Los Angeles,
because of excessive residues of DDT and related insecticides. Insecticides
draining off agricultural lands into the Bay-Delta area have caused levels of DDT
which exceed the amount allowed by the FDA to appear in the bodies of
striped bass and sturgeon. It is possible that the recent decline in San Francisco
Bay crabs may be due to the same cause. Spreading through the food chain,
DDT has begun to cause disastrous declines in the population of birds of prey,
and there is some evidence that gulls are being affected as well. The latter
would extend the web of disaster even further, for the gulls are vital in
controlling waste in shoreline waters.

Now let me follow the track of environmental disaster from the farm to the
cities of California. Again, nitrogen is a valuable guide, this time, surprisingly
enough, to the smog problem. This problem originates with the production
of nitrogen oxides by gasoline engines. Released to the air, these oxides, upon
absorption of sunlight, react with waste hydrocarbon fuel to produce the
noxious constituents of smog. This problem is the direct outcome of the
technological *improvement* of gasoline engines: the development of the modern
high-compression engine. Such engines operate at higher temperatures than
older ones; at these elevated temperatures the oxygen and nitrogen of the
air taken into the engine tend to combine rapidly, with the resultant production
of nitrogen oxides. Once released into the air, nitrogen oxides are activated
by sunlight. They then react with waste hydrocarbon fuel, forming eventually the
notorious PAN—the toxic agent of the smog made famous by Los Angeles.

The present smog-control technique—reduction of waste fuel emission—by
diminishing the interaction of nitrogen oxides with hydrocarbon wastes,
enhances the level of airborne nitrogen oxides, which are themselves
toxic substances. In the air, nitrogen oxides are readily converted to nitrates,
which are then brought down by rain and snow to the land and surface
waters. There they add to the growing burden of nitrogen fertilizer, which, as I
have already indicated, is an important aspect of water pollution. What is
surprising is the amount of nitrogen oxides that are generated by automotive
traffic: more than one-third of the nitrogen contained in the fertilizer currently
employed on U.S. farms. One calculation shows that farms in New Jersey
receive about 25 pounds of nitrogen fertilizer per year (a significant amount
in agricultural practice) from the trucks and cars that travel the New Jersey
highways. Another recent study shows that in the heavily populated eastern
section of the country, the nitrate content of local rainfall is proportional to the
local rate of gasoline consumption.

Thus, the emergence of a new technology—the modern gasoline engine—is
itself responsible for most of the smog problem and for an appreciable part
of the pollution of surface waters with nitrate. And no one needs to be

reminded that smog is a serious hazard to health. Again we see the endless web
of environmental processes at work. Get the engines too hot—for the sake
of generating the power needed to drive a huge car at destructive speeds—and
you set off a chain of events that keeps kids off the playground, sends older
people to a premature death, and, in passing, adds to the already
excessive burden of water pollutants.

This is some of the tragic destruction that lies hidden in the great panorama
of the changing California environment—costs to the people of the state that
do not appear as entries in the balance sheets of industry and agriculture.
These are some of the great debts which must be paid if the state's environment
is to be saved from ultimate destruction. The debts are so embedded in
every feature of the state's economy that it is almost impossible to calculate
them. Their scale, at least, can be secured from the figure produced for the water
quality-control system which will transfer the pollution problem of the Bay-Delta
area to the ocean: $5 billion over 50 years, and continuing at $100 million
a year.

At what cost can the smog that envelops Los Angeles be cleared up—as it
surely must if the city is to survive? Start with the price of rolling back
air pollution that risks the health and well-being of the citizens of the Bay area,
the Peninsula, and San Diego. And do not neglect the damage already done
by smog to the pine forests in the area of Lake Arrowhead. Nitrogen oxides have
just been detected in Yosemite Park; what will it cost if the state's magnificent
forests begin to die, unleashing enormous flood problems? How shall we
reckon the cost of the huge redwoods on the North Coast, which need for their
secure footing the soil built up around their roots during annual floods,
when these floods are stopped by the new dams and the trees begin to topple?
How shall we determine the cost of the urban spread which has covered
the richest soil in the state? What will it cost to restore this soil to agriculture
when the state is forced to limit intensive, pollution-generating fertilization, and
new lands have to be used to sustain food production? What is the price
of those massive walls of concrete, those freeways, which slice across the land,
disrupting drainage patterns and upsetting the delicate balance of forces
that keeps the land from sliding into ravines? Against the value of the new
real-estate developments on landfills in San Francisco Bay, calculate the cost of
the resulting changes in tidal movements, which have decreased the dilution
of the polluting nutrients by fresh water from the sea and have worsened
the algal overgrowths. Or balance against the value of the offshore oil the cost of
a constant risk of beach and ocean pollution until the offending wells are
pumped dry. Finally, figure, if possible, what it will cost to restore the natural
fertility of the soil in central California, to keep the nitrogen in the soil,
where it belongs, and to develop a new, more mixed form of agriculture that
will make it possible to get rid of most insecticides and make better use of
the natural biological controls.

If the magnitude of the state's environmental problems is staggering, perhaps
there is some consolation in the fact that California is not alone. Most of Lake
Erie has been lost to pollution. In Illinois, every major river has been
overburdened with fertilizer drainage and has lost its powers of self-purification.

Automobile smog hangs like a pall over even Denver and Phoenix. Every major city is experiencing worsening air pollution. The entire nation is in the grip of the environmental crisis.

What is to be done? What *can* be done? Although we are, I believe, on a path which can only lead to self-destruction, I am also convinced that we have not yet passed the point of no return. We have time—perhaps a generation—in which to save the environment from the final effects of the violence we have already done to it, and to save ourselves from our own suicidal folly. But this is a very short time to achieve the massive environmental repair that is needed. We will need to start, now, on a new path. And the first action is to recognize how badly we have gone wrong in the use of the environment and to mobilize every available resource for the huge task of saving it.

Yet all the marvelous knowledge in our universities and laboratories seems now to stand helpless, while the air becomes fouler every day, beaches covered with oil, and precious water and soil more heavily laden with pollutants.

But there is another crisis—one that has struck the nation's entire scientific community. This crisis, like the environmental one, is also man-made and disastrously short-sighted; it is the drastic curtailment of the funds for research and education.

What a tragedy! At the very moment that the nation has begun to sense the urgency of the environmental crisis, when the first steps in the large and urgent task must be taken in the laboratories and classrooms of our universities, the tools are denied the men who would use them.

The huge undertakings listed here cannot even be begun unless we drastically reorganize our priorities. We cannot continue to devote the talent of our engineers and the competence of our workers to the production of overpowered, pollution-generating cars that do violence on the road and in the ecosystem. We cannot burden our productive resources with a monstrous device like the SST—which, if used in the U.S., will bring the violence of airport noise to 60 million Americans. We cannot continue to waste manpower and resources on weapons that become obsolete before they are produced—and which, if ever used, will destroy this planet as a place for human life. In a crisis of survival, business as usual is suicide.

The environmental crisis has brought us to a great turning point in this nation's history. We have become a nation that wields the greatest power in the history of man: power in the form of food, industrial plants, vehicles, and the weapons of war. We have also become a nation beset by violence: on the battlefield, on the highways, in personal encounters, and, more fundamentally, in the destruction of the natural, harmonious fabric of the environmental system which supports us. It is this fundamental violence to the world in which we live which divides us, as we compete among ourselves for the earth's goods, unaware that each of us, in our own way, is thereby contributing to the destruction of the whole that supports us all.

The time has come to forge a great alliance in this nation: All of us now know that if we are to survive, the environment must be maintained as a balanced, harmonious whole. We must all work together to preserve it. If we fail, we shall abandon the place where we must live—the thin skin of air, water, soil, and living things on the planet Earth—to destruction. The obligation which our technological society forces upon all of us, young and old, black and white, right and left, scientist and citizen alike, is to discover how humanity can survive the new power which science has given it. Every major advance in the technological competence of man has enforced new obligations on human society. The present age of technology is no exception to this rule of history. We already know the enormous benefits it can bestow, and we have begun to perceive its frightful threats. The crisis generated by this knowledge is upon us.

We are enormously fortunate that our young people—the first generation to carry strontium 90 in their bones and DDT in their fat—have become particularly sensitive to this ominous paradox of the modern world. For it is they who face the frightful task of seeking humane knowledge in a world which has, with cunning perversity, transformed the power that knowledge generates into an instrument of catastrophe.

The environmental crisis is a grim challenge. It also is a great opportunity. From it we may yet learn that the proper use of science is not to conquer nature, but to live in it. We may yet learn that to save ourselves we must save the world that is our habitat. We may yet discover how to devote the wisdom of science and the power of technology to the welfare, the survival of man.

eight
american
institutions and
ecological
ideals

LEO MARX

*Leo Marx (b. 1919), a leading academic exponent of
American Studies, received his doctorate from Harvard
University and has been on the faculty of Amherst College
since 1958. His* Machine in the Garden *(1964) described
at length the impact of technology on American writers
and artists, and the essay reproduced here couples this
previous work with concerns over whether any sort of
ecological ideal has hope of fulfillment within the
framework of America's national character.*

Anyone familiar with the work of the classic American
writers (I am thinking of men like Cooper, Emerson,
Thoreau, Melville, Whitman, and Mark Twain) is likely to
have developed an interest in what we recently have
learned to call ecology. One of the first things we associate
with each of the writers just named is a distinctive,
vividly particularized setting (or landscape) inseparable
from the writer's conception of man. Partly because of the
special geographic and political circumstances of American
experience, and partly because they were influenced by the
romantic vision of man's relations with nature, all of the
writers mentioned possessed a heightened sense of
place. Yet words like *place, landscape,* or *setting* scarcely

Source: Leo Marx, "American Institutions and Ecological Ideals,"
Science 170 (November 27, 1970): 945–52. Copyright © 1970
by the American Association for the Advancement of Science.
Reprinted by permission of the author and the publisher.

can do justice to the significance these writers imparted to external nature in their work. They took for granted a thorough and delicate interpenetration of consciousness and environment. In fact it now seems evident that these gifted writers had begun, more than a century ago, to measure the quality of American life against something like an ecological ideal.

The ideal I have in mind, quite simply, is the maintenance of a healthy life-enhancing interaction between man and the environment. This is layman's language for the proposition that every organism, in order to avoid extinction or expulsion from its ecosystem, must conform to certain minimal requirements of that system. What makes the concept of the ecosystem difficult to grasp, admittedly, is the fact that the boundaries between systems are always somewhat indistinct, and our technology is making them less distinct all the time. Since an ecosystem includes not only all living organisms (plants and animals) but also the inorganic (physical and chemical) components of the environment, it has become extremely difficult, in the thermonuclear age, to verify even the relatively limited autonomy of local or regional systems. If a decision taken in Moscow or Washington can effect a catastrophic change in the chemical composition of the entire biosphere, then the idea of a San Francisco, or Bay Area, or California, or even North American ecosystem loses much of its clarity and force. Similar difficulties arise when we contemplate the global rate of human population growth. All this is only to say that, on ecological grounds, the case for world government is beyond argument. Meanwhile, we have no choice but to use the nation-states as political instruments for coping with the rapid deterioration of the physical world we inhabit.

The chief question before us, then, is this: What are the prospects, given the character of America's dominant institutions, for the fulfillment of this ecological ideal? But first, what is the significance of the current "environmental crusade"? Why should we be skeptical about its efficacy? How shall we account for the curious response of the scientific community? To answer these questions I will attempt to characterize certain of our key institutions from an ecological perspective. I want to suggest the striking convergence of the scientific and the literary criticism of our national life-style. In conclusion I will suggest a few responses to the ecological crisis indicated by that scientific-literary critique.

LIMITS OF CONSERVATIONIST THOUGHT

In this country, until recently, ecological thinking has been obscured by the more popular, if limited, conservationist viewpoint. Because our government seldom accorded protection of the environment a high priority, much of the responsibility for keeping that end in view fell upon a few voluntary organizations known as the "conservation movement." From the beginning the movement attracted people with enough time and money to enjoy the outdoor life: sportsmen, naturalists (both amateur and professional), and of course property owners anxious to protect the sanctity of their rural or wilderness retreats. As a result, the conservationist cause came to be identified with the special interests of a few private citizens. It seldom, if ever, has been made to seem pertinent to the welfare of the poor, the nonwhite population, or, for that matter, the great majority of urban Americans. The environment that mattered most to conservationists was the environment beyond the city limits. Witness the names of such leading organizations as the Sierra Club, the National Wildlife Federation, the Audubon Society, and the Izaac Walton League. In the view of many conservationists nature is a world that exists apart from, and for the benefit of, mankind.

The ecological perspective is quite different. Its philosophic root is the secular idea that man (including his works—the secondary, or man-made, environment) is wholly and ineluctably embedded in the tissue of natural process. The interconnections are delicate, infinitely complex, never to be severed. If this organic (or holistic) view of nature has not been popular, it is partly because it calls into question many presuppositions of our culture. Even today an excessive interest in this idea of nature carries, as it did in Emerson's and in Jefferson's time, a strong hint of irregularity and possible subversion. (Nowadays it is associated with the antibourgeois defense of the environment expounded by the long-haired "cop-outs" of the youth movement.) Partly in order to counteract these dangerously idealistic notions, American conservationists often have made a point of seeming hardheaded, which is to say, "realistic" or practical. When their aims have been incorporated in national political programs, notably during the administrations of the two Roosevelts, the emphasis has been upon the efficient use of resources under the supervision of well-trained technicians. Whatever the achievements of such programs, as implemented by the admirable if narrowly defined work of such agencies as the National Park Service, the U.S. Forest Service, or the Soil Conservation Service, they did not raise the kinds of questions about our overall capacity for survival that are brought into view by ecology. In this sense, conservationist thought is pragmatic and meliorist in tenor, whereas ecology is, in the purest meaning of the word, radical.

The relative popularity of the conservation movement helps to explain why troubled scientists, many of whom foresaw the scope and gravity of the environmental crisis a long while ago, have had such a difficult time arousing their countrymen. As early as 1864 George Perkins Marsh, sometimes said to be the father of American ecology, warned that the earth was "fast becoming an unfit home for its noblest inhabitant," and that unless men changed their ways it would be reduced "to such a condition of impoverished productiveness, of shattered surface, of climatic excess, as to threaten the depravation, barbarism, and perhaps even extinction of the species." No one was listening to Marsh in 1864, and some 80 years later, according to a distinguished naturalist who tried to convey a similar warning, most Americans still were not listening. "It is amazing," wrote Fairfield Osborn in 1948, "how far one has to travel to find a person, even among the widely informed, who is aware of the processes of mounting destruction that we are inflicting upon our life sources."

THE ENVIRONMENT CRUSADE, CIRCA 1969

But that was 1948, and, as we all know, the situation now is wholly changed.
Toward the end of the 1960's there was a sudden upsurge of public interest in
the subject. The devastation of the environment and the threat of overpopulation
became too obvious to be ignored. A sense of anxiety close to panic seized
many people, including politicians and leaders of the communications industry.
The mass media began to spread the alarm. Television gave prime coverage to
a series of relatively minor yet visually sensational ecological disasters.
Once again, as in the coverage of the Vietnam War, the close-up power of the
medium was demonstrated. The sight of lovely beaches covered with crude
oil, hundreds of dead and dying birds trapped in the viscous stuff, had an
incalculable effect upon a mass audience. After years of indifference, the press
suddenly decided that the jeremiads of naturalists might be important news,
and a whole new vocabulary (*environment, ecology, balance of nature,
population explosion,* and so on) entered common speech. Meanwhile, the
language of reputable scientists was escalating to a pitch of excitement
comparable with that of the most fervent young radicals. Barry Commoner, for
example, gave a widely reported speech describing the deadly pollution of
California water reserves as a result of the excessive use of nitrates as fertilizer.
This method of increasing agricultural productivity, he said, is so disruptive
of the chemical balance of soil and water that within a generation it could
poison irreparably the water supply of the whole area. The *New York Times* ran
the story under the headline: "Ecologist Sees U.S. on Suicidal Course." But
it was the demographers and population biologists, worried about behavior
even less susceptible to regulatory action, who used the most portentous
rhetoric. "We must realize that unless we are extremely lucky," Paul Ehrlich
told an audience in the summer of 1969, "everybody will disappear in a
cloud of blue steam in 20 years."

To a layman who assumes that responsible scientists choose their words with
care, this kind of talk is bewildering. How seriously should he take it?
He realizes, of course, that he has no way, on his own, to evaluate the factual
or scientific basis for these fearful predictions. But the scientific community, to
which he naturally turns, is not much help. While most scientists calmly go
about their business, activists like Commoner and Ehrlich dominate the
headlines. (One could cite the almost equally gloomy forecasts of Harrison
Brown, George Wald, René Dubos, and a dozen other distinguished scholars.)
When Anthony Lewis asked a "leading European biologist" the same question—
how seriously should one take this idea of the imminent extinction of the
race?—the scholar smiled, Lewis reports, and said, "I suppose we have between
35 and 100 years before the end of life on earth." No—what is bewildering
is the disparity between words and action, between the all-too-credible prophecy
of disaster and the response—or rather the nonresponse—of the organized
scientific community. From a layman's viewpoint, the professional scientific
organizations would seem to have an obligation here—where nothing less than
human survival is in question—either to endorse or to correct the pronouncements
of their distinguished colleagues. If a large number of scientists do indeed

endorse the judgment of the more vociferous ecologists, then the inescapable
question is: What are they doing about it? Why do they hesitate to use the
concerted prestige and force of their profession to effect radical changes
in national policy and behavior? How is it that most scientists, in the face of this
awful knowledge, if indeed it is knowledge, are able to carry on business
more or less as usual? One might have expected them to raise their voices,
activate their professional organizations, petition the Congress, send delegations
to the President, and speak out to the people and the government. Why, in
short, are they not mounting a campaign of education and political action?

WHY ARE MOST SCIENTISTS UNDISTURBED?

The most plausible answer seems to be that many scientists, like many of their
fellow citizens, are ready to believe that such a campaign already has begun. And
if, indeed, one accepts the version of political reality disseminated by the
communications industry, they are correct: the campaign *has* begun. By the
summer of 1969 it had become evident that the media were preparing to give
the ecological crisis the kind of saturation treatment accorded the civil rights
movement in the early 1960's and the anti-Vietnam War protest after that.
(Observers made this comparison from the beginning.) Much of the tone and
substance of the campaign was set by the advertising business. Thus, a
leading teen-age magazine, *Seventeen,* took a full-page ad in the *New York Times*
to announce, beneath a picture of a handsome collegiate couple strolling
meditatively through autumn leaves, "The environment crusade emphasizes
the fervent concerns of the young with our nation's 'quality of life.' Their voices
impel us to act now on the mushrooming problems of conservation and
ecology." A more skeptical voice might impel us to think about the Madison
Avenue strategists who had recognized a direct new path into the lucrative youth
market. The "crusade," as they envisaged it, was to be a bland, well-mannered,
clean-up campaign, conducted in the spirit of an adolescent love affair and
nicely timed to deflect student attention from the disruptive political issues of
the 1960's. A national survey of college students confirmed this hope.
"Environment May Eclipse Vietnam as College Issue," the makers of the
survey reported, and one young man's comment seemed to sum up their findings:
"A lot of people are becoming disenchanted with the antiwar movement,"
he said. "People who are frustrated and disillusioned are starting to turn to
ecology." On New Year's Day 1970, the President of the United States joined
the crusade. Adapting the doomsday rhetoric of the environmentalists to his
own purposes, he announced that "the nineteen-seventies absolutely must
be the years when America pays its debt to the past by reclaiming the purity of
its air, its waters and our living environment. It is literally now or never."

Under the circumstances, it is understandable that most scientists, like most
other people (except for the disaffected minority of college students),
have been largely unresponsive to the alarmist rhetoric of the more panicky
environmentalists. The campaign to save the environment no longer seems to need
their help. Not only have the media been awakened, and with them a large
segment of the population, but the President himself, along with many

government officials, has been enlisted in the cause. On 10 February 1970, President Nixon sent a special message to the Congress outlining a comprehensive 37-point program of action against pollution. Is it any wonder that the mood at recent meetings of conservationists has become almost cheerful—as if the movement, at long last, really had begun to move? After all, the grim forecasts of the ecologists necessarily have been couched in conditional language, thus: *If* California farmers continue their excessive use of nitrates, *then* the water supply will be irreparably poisoned. But now that the facts have been revealed, and with so much government activity in prospect, may we not assume that disaster will be averted? There is no need, therefore, to take the alarmists seriously—which is only to say that most scientists still have confidence in the capacity of our political leaders, and of our institutions, to cope with the crisis.

But is that confidence warranted by the current "crusade"? Many observers have noted that the President's message was strong in visionary language and weak in substance. He recommended no significant increase in funds needed to implement the program. Coming from a politician with a well-known respect for strategies based on advertising and public relations, this high-sounding talk should make us wary. Is it designed to protect the environment or to assuage anxiety or to distract the antiwar movement or to provide the cohesive force necessary for national unity behind the Republican administration? How can we distinguish the illusion of activity fostered by the media—and the President— from auguries of genuine action? On this score, the frequently invoked parallel of the civil rights and the antiwar movements should give us pause. For, while each succeeded in focusing attention upon a dangerous situation, it is doubtful whether either got us very far along toward the elimination of the danger. At first each movement won spectacular victories, but now, in retrospect, they too look more like ideological than substantive gains. In many ways the situation of blacks in America is more desperate in 1970 than it was in 1960. Similarly, the war in Southeast Asia, far from having been stopped by the peace movement, now threatens to encompass other countries and to continue indefinitely. This is not to imply that the strenuous efforts to end the war or to eradicate racism have been bootless. Some day the whole picture may well look quite different; we may look back on the 1960's as the time when a generation was prepared for a vital transformation of American society.

Nevertheless, scientists would do well to contemplate the example of these recent protest movements. They would be compelled to recognize, for one thing, that, while public awareness may be indispensable for effecting changes in national policy, it hardly guarantees results. In retrospect, indeed, the whole tenor of the civil rights and antiwar campaigns now seems much too optimistic. Neither program took sufficient account of the deeply entrenched, institutionalized character of the collective behavior it aimed to change. If leaders of the campaign to save the environment were to make the same kind of error, it would not be surprising. A certain innocent trust in the efficacy of words, propaganda, and rational persuasion always has characterized the conservation movement in this country. Besides, there is a popular notion that ecological problems are in essence technological, not political, and therefore easier to solve than the problems of racism, war, or imperialism. To indicate why this view is a mistaken one, why in fact it would be folly to discount the urgency of the environmental crisis on these grounds, I now want to consider the fitness of certain dominant American institutions for the fulfillment of the ecological ideal.

THE DYNAMISM OF AMERICA

Seen from an ecological perspective, a salient characteristic of American society is its astonishing dynamism. Ever since the first European settlements were established on the Atlantic seaboard, our history has been one of virtually uninterrupted expansion. How many decades, if any, have there been since 1607 when this society failed to expand its population, territory, and economic power? When foreigners speak of Americanization they invariably have in mind this dynamic, expansionary, unrestrained behavior. "No sooner do you set foot upon American ground," wrote de Tocqueville, "than you are stunned by a kind of tumult; a confused clamor is heard on every side, and a thousand simultaneous voices demand the satisfaction of their social wants. Everything is in motion around you. . . ." To be sure, a majority of these clamorous people were of European origin, and their most effective instrument for the transformation of the wilderness—their science and technology—was a product of Western culture. But the unspoiled terrain of North America gave European dynamism a peculiar effervescence. The seemingly unlimited natural resources and the relative absence of cultural or institutional restraints made possible what surely has been the fastest-developing, most mobile, most relentlessly innovative society in world history. By now that dynamism inheres in every aspect of our lives, from the dominant national ethos to the structure of our economic institutions down to the deportment of individuals.

The ideological counterpart to the nation's physical expansion has been its celebration of quantity. What has been valued most in American popular culture is growth, development, size (bigness), and—by extension—change, novelty, innovation, wealth, and power. This tendency was noted a long while ago, especially by foreign travelers, but only recently have historians begun to appreciate the special contribution of Christianity to this quantitative, expansionary ethos. The crux here is the aggressive, man-centered attitude toward the environment fostered by Judeo-Christian thought: everything in nature, living or inorganic, exists to serve man. For only man can hope (by joining God) to transcend nature. According to one historian of science, Lynn White, the dynamic thrust of Western science and technology derives in large measure from this Christian emphasis, unique among the great world religions, upon the separation of man from nature.

But one need not endorse White's entire argument to recognize that Americans, from the beginning, found in the Bible a divine sanction for their violent assault upon the physical environment. To the Puritans of New England, the New World landscape was Satan's territory, a hideous wilderness inhabited by the unredeemed and fit chiefly for conquest. What moral precept could have served their purpose better than the Lord's injunction to be fruitful and multiply and subdue the earth and exercise dominion over every living creature? Then, too, the millennial cast of evangelical protestantism made even more dramatic the notion that this earth, and everything upon it, is an expendable support system for man's voyage to eternity. Later, as industrialization gained momentum, the emphasis shifted from the idea of nature as the devil's country to the idea of nature as commodity. When the millennial hope was secularized, and salvation was replaced by the goal of economic and social progress, it became possible to quantify the rate of human improvement. In our time this quantifying bent reached its logical end with the enshrinement of the gross national product— one all-encompassing index of the state of the union itself.

Perhaps the most striking thing about this expansionary ethos, from an ecological viewpoint, has been its capacity to supplant a whole range of commonsense notions about man's relations with nature which are recognized by some preliterate peoples and are implicit in the behavior of certain animal species. These include the ideas that natural resources are exhaustible, that the unchecked growth of a species will eventually lead to its extinction, and that other organisms may have a claim to life worthy of respect.

THE EXPANSIONARY SYSTEM

The record of American business, incomparably successful according to quantitative economic measures like the gross national product, also looks quite different when viewed from an ecological perspective. Whereas the environmental ideal I have been discussing affirms the need for each organism to observe limits set by its ecosystem, the whole thrust of industrial capitalism has been in the opposite direction: it has placed the highest premium upon ingenious methods for circumventing those limits. After comparing the treatment that various nations have accorded their respective portions of the earth, Fairfield Osborn said this of the United States: "The story of our nation in the last century as regards the use of forests, grasslands, wildlife and water sources is the most violent and the most destructive in the long history of civilization." If that estimate is just, a large part of the credit must be given to an economic system unmatched in calling forth man's profit-making energies. By the same token, it is a system that does pitifully little to encourage or reward those constraints necessary for the long-term ecological well-being of society. Consider, for example, the fate of prime agricultural lands on the borders of our burgeoning cities. What happens when a landowner is offered a small fortune by a developer? What agency protects the public interest from the irretrievable loss of topsoil that requires centuries to produce? Who sees to it that housing, factories, highways, and shopping centers are situated on the far more plentiful sites where nothing edible ever will grow? The answer is that no such agencies exist, and the market principle is allowed to rule. Since World War II approximately one-fifth of California's invaluable farm land has been lost in this way. Here, as in many cases of air and water pollution, the dominant motive of our business system—private profit— leads to the violation of ecological standards.

Early in the industrial era one might reasonably have expected, as Thorstein Veblen did, that the scientific and technological professions, with their strong bent toward rationality and efficiency, would help to control the ravening economic appetites whetted by America's natural abundance. Veblen assumed that well-trained technicians, engineers, and scientists would be repelled by the wastefulness of the business system. He therefore looked to them for leadership in shaping alternatives to a culture obsessed with "conspicuous consumption." But, so far, that leadership has not appeared. On the contrary, this new technical elite, with its commitment to highly specialized, value-free research, has enthusiastically placed its skill in the service of business and military enterprise. This is one reason, incidentally, why today's rebellious young are unimpressed by the claim that the higher learning entails a commitment to rationality. They see our best-educated, most "rational" elite serving what strikes them as a higher irrationality. So far from providing a counterforce to the business system, the scientific and technological professions in fact have strengthened the ideology of American corporate capitalism, including its large armaments sector, by bringing to it their high-minded faith in the benign consequences of the most rapidly accelerating rate of technological innovation attainable.

But not only are we collectively committed, as a nation, to the idea of continuing growth; each subordinate unit of the society holds itself to a similar standard of success. Each state, city, village, and neighborhood; each corporation, independent merchant, and voluntary organization; each ethnic group, family, and child—each person—should, ideally speaking, strive for growth. Translated into ecological terms, this popular measure of success—becoming bigger, richer, more powerful—means gaining control over more and more of the available resources. When resources were thought to be inexhaustible, as they were thought to be throughout most of our national history, the release of these unbounded entrepreneurial energies was considered an aspect of individual liberation. And so it was, at least for large segments of the population. But today, when that assumption no longer makes sense, those energies are still being generated. It is as if a miniaturized version of the nation's expansionary ethos had been implanted in every citizen—not excluding the technicians and scientists. And when we consider the extremes to which the specialization of function has been carried in the sciences, each expert working his own miniscule sector of the knowledge industry, it is easier to account for the unresponsiveness of the scientific community to the urgent warnings of alarmed ecologists. If most scientists and engineers seem not to be listening, much less acting, it is because these highly skilled men are so busy doing what every good American is supposed to do.

On the other hand, it is not surprising that a clever novelist like Norman Mailer, or a popular interpreter of science like Rachel Carson, or an imaginative medical researcher like Alan Gregg each found it illuminating in recent years to compare the unchecked growth of American society, with all the resulting disorder, to the haphazard spread of cancer cells in a living organism. There is nothing new, of course, about the analogy between the social order and the human body; the conceit has a long history in literature. Since the early 1960's, however, Mailer has been invoking the more specific idea of America as a carcinogenic environment. Like any good poetic figure, this one has a basis in fact. Not only does it call to mind the radioactive matter we have deposited in the earth and the sea, or the work of such allegedly cancer-producing enterprises as the tobacco and automobile industries, or the effects of some of the new drugs administered by doctors in recent years, but, even more subtly, it reminds us of the parallel between cancer and our expansionary national ethos, which, like a powerful ideological hormone, stimulates the reckless, uncontrolled growth of each cell in the social organism.

In the interests of historical accuracy and comprehensiveness, needless to say, all of these sweeping generalizations would have to be extensively qualified. The record is rich in accounts of determined, troubled Americans who have criticized and actively resisted the nation's expansionary abandon. A large part of our governmental apparatus was created in order to keep these acquisitive, self-aggrandizing energies within tolerable limits. And of course the full story would acknowledge the obvious benefits, especially the individual freedom and prosperity, many Americans owe to the very dynamism that now threatens our survival. But in this brief compass my aim is to emphasize that conception of man's relation to nature which, so far as we can trace its consequences, issued in the *dominant* forms of national behavior. And that is a largely one-sided story. It is a story, moreover, to which our classic American writers, to their inestimable credit, have borne eloquent witness. If there is a single native institution which has consistently criticized American life from a vantage like that of ecology, it is the institution of letters.

AMERICA'S PASTORAL LITERATURE

A notable fact about imaginative literature in America, when viewed from an ecological perspective, is the number of our most admired works written in obedience to a pastoral impulse. By "pastoral impulse" I mean the urge, in the face of society's increasing power and complexity, to retreat in the direction of nature. The most obvious form taken by this withdrawal from the world of established institutions is a movement in space. The writer or narrator describes, or a character enacts, a move away from a relatively sophisticated to a simpler, more "natural" environment. Whether this new setting is an unspoiled wilderness, like Cooper's forests and plains, Melville's remote Pacific, Faulkner's Big Woods, or Hemingway's Africa, or whether it is as tame as Emerson's New England village common, Thoreau's Walden Pond, or Robert Frost's pasture, its significance derives from the plain fact that it is "closer" to nature: it is a landscape that bears fewer marks of human intervention.

This symbolic action, which reenacts the initial transit of Europeans to North America, may be understood in several ways, and no one of them can do it justice. To begin with, there is an undeniable element of escapism about this familiar, perhaps universal, desire to get away from the imperatives of a complicated social life. No one has conveyed this feeling with greater economy or simplicity than Robert Frost in the first line of his poem "Directive": "Back out of all this now too much for us." Needless to say, if our literary pastoralism lent expression only to this escapist impulse, we would be compelled to call it self-indulgent, puerile, or regressive.

But fortunately this is not the case. In most American pastorals the movement toward nature also may be understood as a serious criticism, explicit or implied, of the established social order. It calls into question a society dominated by a mechanistic system of value, keyed to perfecting the routine means of existence, yet oblivious to its meaning and purpose. We recall Thoreau's description, early in *Walden,* of the lives of quiet desperation led by his Concord neighbors, or the first pages of Melville's *Moby Dick,* with Ishmael's account of his moods of suicidal depression as he contemplates the meaningless work required of the inhabitants of Manhattan Island. At one time this critical attitude toward the workaday life was commonly dismissed as aristocratic or elitist. We said that it could speak only for a leisure class for whom deprivation was no problem. But today, in a society with the technological capacity to supply everyone with an adequate standard of living, that objection has lost most of its force. The necessary conditions for giving a decent livelihood to every citizen no longer include harder work, increased productivity, or endless technological innovation. But of course such an egalitarian economic program would entail a more equitable distribution of wealth, and the substitution of economic sufficiency for the goal of an endlessly "rising" standard of living. The mere fact that such possibilities exist explains why our literary pastorals, which blur distinctions between the economic, moral, and esthetic flaws of society, now seem more cogent. In the 19th century, many pastoralists, like today's radical ecologists, saw the system as potentially destructive in its innermost essence. Their dominant figure for industrial society, with its patent confusion about ends and means, was the social machine. Our economy is the kind of system, said Thoreau, where men become the tools of their tools.

Of course, there is nothing particularly American about this pessimistic literary response to industrialism. Since the romantic movement it has been a dominant theme of all Western literature. Most gifted writers have expended a large share of their energy in an effort to discover—or, more precisely, to imagine— alternatives to the way of life that emerged with the industrial revolution. The difference is that in Europe there was a range of other possible life-styles which had no counterpart in this country. There were enclaves of preindustrial culture (provincial, esthetic, religious, aristocratic) which retained their vitality long after the bourgeois revolutions, and there also was a new, revolutionary, urban working class. This difference, along with the presence in America of a vast, rich, unspoiled landscape, helps to explain the exceptionally strong hold of the pastoral motive upon the native imagination. If our writers conceived of life from something like an ecological perspective, it is largely because of their heightened sensitivity to the unspoiled environment, and man's relation to it, as the basis for an alternative to the established social order.

What, then, can we learn about possible alternatives from our pastoral literature? The difficulty here lies in the improbability which surrounds the affirmative content of the pastoral retreat. In the typical American fable the high point of the withdrawal toward nature is an idyllic interlude which gains a large measure of its significance from the sharp contrast with the everyday, "real," world. This is an evanescent moment of peace and contentment when the writer (or narrator, or protagonist) enjoys a sense of integration with the surrounding environment that approaches ecstatic fulfillment. It is often a kind of visionary experience, couched in a language of such intense, extreme, even mystical feeling that it is difficult for many readers (though not, significantly, for adherents of today's youth culture) to take it seriously. But it is important to keep in view some of the reasons for this literary extravagance. In a commercial, optimistic, self-satisfied culture, it was not easy for writers to make an alternate mode of experience credible. Their problem was to endow an ideal vision— some would call it utopian—with enough sensual authenticity to carry readers beyond the usual, conventionally accepted limits of commonsense reality. Nevertheless, the pastoral interlude, rightly understood, does have a bearing upon the choices open to a postindustrial society. It must be taken, not as representing a program to be copied, but as a symbolic action which embodies values, attitudes, modes of thought and feeling alternative to those which characterize the dynamic, expansionary life-style of modern America.

The focus of our literary pastoralism, accordingly, is upon a contrast between two environments representing virtually all aspects of man's relation to nature. In place of the aggressive thrust of 19th-century capitalism, the pastoral interlude exemplifies a far more restrained, accommodating kind of behavior. The chief goal is not, as Alexander Hamilton argued it was, to enhance the nation's corporate wealth and power; rather it is the Jeffersonian "pursuit of happiness." In economic terms, then, pastoralism entails a distinction between a commitment to unending growth and the concept of material sufficiency. The aim of the pastoral economy is *enough*—enough production and consumption to insure a decent quality of life. Jefferson's dislike of industrialization was based on this standard; he was bent on the subordination of quantitative to qualitative "standards of living."

From a psychological viewpoint, the pastoral retreat affirmed the possibility of maintaining man's mental equilibrium by renewed emphasis upon his inner needs. The psychic equivalent of the balance of nature (in effect the balance of *human* nature) is a more or less equal capacity to cope with external and internal sources of anxiety. In a less-developed landscape, according to these fables, behavior can be more free, spontaneous, authentic—in a word, more natural. The natural in psychic experience refers to activities of mind which are inborn or somehow primary. Whether we call them intuitive, unconscious, or preconscious, the significant fact is that they do not have to be learned or deliberately acquired. By contrast, then, the expansionary society is figured forth as dangerously imbalanced on the side of those rational faculties conducive to the manipulation of the physical environment. We think of Melville's Ahab, in whom the specialization of function induces a peculiar kind of power-obsessed, if technically competent, mentality. "My means are sane," he says, "my motive and my object mad."

This suspicion of the technical, highly trained intellect comports with the emphasis in our pastoral literature upon those aspects of life that are common to all men. Whereas the industrial society encourages and rewards the habit of mind which analyzes, separates, categorizes, and makes distinctions, the felicity enjoyed during the pastoral interlude is a tacit tribute to the opposite habit. This kind of pleasure derives from the connection-making, analogizing, poetic imagination—one that aspires to a unified conception of reality. At the highest or metaphysical level of abstraction, then, romantic pastoralism is holistic. During the more intense pastoral interludes, an awareness of the entire environment, extending to the outer reaches of the cosmos, affects the perception of each separate thing, idea, event. In place of the technologically efficient but limited concept of nature as a body of discrete manipulatable objects, our pastoral literature presents an organic conception of man's relation to his environment.

A CONVERGENCE OF INSIGHTS

What I am trying to suggest is the striking convergence of the literary and the ecological views of America's dominant institutions. Our literature contains a deep intuition of the gathering environmental crisis and its causes. To be sure, the matter-of-fact idiom of scientific ecology may not be poetic or inspiring. Instead of conveying Wordsworthian impulses from the vernal wood, it reports the rate at which monoxide poisoning is killing the trees. Nevertheless, the findings of ecologists confirm the indictment of the self-aggrandizing way of life that our leading writers have been building up for almost two centuries. In essence it is an indictment of the destructive, power-oriented uses to which we put scientific and technological knowledge. The philosophic source of this dangerous behavior is an arrogant conception of man, and above all of human consciousness, as wholly unique—as an entity distinct from, and potentially independent of, the rest of nature.

As for the alternative implied by the pastoral retreat, it also anticipates certain insights of ecology. Throughout this body of imaginative writing, the turn toward nature is represented as a means of gaining access to governing values, meanings, and purposes. In the past, to be sure, many readers found the escapist, sentimental overtones of this motive embarrassing. As a teacher, I can testify that, until recently, many pragmatically inclined students were put off by the obscurely metaphysical, occultish notions surrounding the idea of harmony with nature. It lacked specificity. But now all that is changing. The current environmental crisis has in a sense put a literal, factual, often quantifiable base under this poetic idea. Nature as a transmitter of signals and a dictator of choices now is present to us in the quite literal sense that the imbalance of an ecosystem, when scientifically understood, defines certain precise limits to human behavior. We are told, for example, that if we continue contaminating Lake Michigan at the present rate, the lake will be "dead" in roughly 10 years. Shall we save the lake or continue allowing the cities and industries which pollute it to reduce expenses and increase profits? As such choices become more frequent, man's relations with nature will in effect be seen to set the limits of various economic, social, and political practices. And the concept of harmonious relations between man and the physical environment, instead of seeming to be a vague projection of human wishes, must come to be respected as a necessary, realistic, limiting goal. This convergence of literary and scientific insight reinforces the naturalistic idea that man, to paraphrase Melville, must eventually lower his conceit of attainable felicity, locating it not in power or transcendence but in a prior need to sustain life itself.

A PROPOSAL AND SOME CONCLUSIONS

Assuming that this sketch of America's dominant institutions as seen from a pastoral-ecological vantage is not grossly inaccurate, what inferences can we draw from it? What bearing does it have upon our current effort to cope with the deterioration of the environment? What special significance does it have for concerned scientists and technologists? I shall draw several conclusions, beginning with a specific recommendation for action by the American Association for the Advancement of Science.

First, then, let me propose that the Association establish a panel of the best qualified scientists, representing as many as possible of the disciplines involved, to serve as a national review board for ecological information. This board would take the responsibility for locating and defining the crucial problems (presumably it would recruit special task forces for specific assignments) and make public recommendations whenever feasible. To be sure, some scientists will be doing a similar job for the government, but, if an informed electorate is to evaluate the government's program, it must have an independent source of knowledge. One probable objection is that scientists often disagree, and feel reluctant to disagree in public. But is this a healthy condition for a democracy? Perhaps the time has come to lift the dangerous veil of omniscience from the world of science and technology. If the experts cannot agree, let them issue minority reports. If our survival is at stake, we should be allowed to know what the problems and the choices are. The point here is not that we laymen look to scientists for *the* answer, or that we expect them to save us. But we do ask for their active involvement in solving problems about which they are the best-informed citizens. Not only should such a topflight panel of scientists be set up on a national basis, but—perhaps more important—similar committees should be set up to help make the best scientific judgment available to the citizens of every state, city, and local community.

But there will also be those who object on the ground that an organization as august as the American Association for the Advancement of Science must not be drawn into politics. The answer, of course, is that American scientists and technologists are now and have always been involved in politics. A profession whose members place their services at the disposal of the government, the military, and the private corporations can hardly claim immunity now. Scientific and technological knowledge unavoidably is used for political purposes. But it also is a national resource. The real question in a democratic society, therefore, is whether that knowledge can be made as available to ordinary voters as it is to those, like the Department of Defense or General Electric, who can most easily buy it. If scientists are worried about becoming partisans, then their best defense is to speak with their own disinterested public voice. To allow the burden of alerting and educating the people to fall upon a few volunteers is a scandal. Scientists, as represented by their professional organizations, have a responsibility to make sure that their skills are used to fulfill as well as to violate the ecological ideal. And who knows? If things get bad enough, the scientific community may take steps to discourage its members from serving the violators.

There is another, perhaps more compelling, reason why scientists and technologists, as an organized professional group, must become more actively involved. It was scientists, after all, who first sounded the alarm. What action we take as a society *and how quickly we take it* depend in large measure upon the credibility of the alarmists. Who is to say, if organized science does not, which alarms we should take seriously? What group has anything like the competence of scientists and technologists to evaluate the evidence? Or, to put it negatively, what group can do more, by mere complacency and inaction, to insure an inadequate response to the environmental crisis? It is a well-known fact that Americans hold the scientific profession in the highest esteem. So long as most scientists go about their business as usual, so long as they seem unperturbed by the urgent appeals of their own colleagues, it is likely that most laymen, including our political representatives, will remain skeptical.

The arguments for the more active involvement of the scientific community in public debate illustrate the all-encompassing and essentially political character of the environmental crisis. If the literary-ecological perspective affords an accurate view, we must eventually take into account the deep-seated, institutional causes of our distress. No cosmetic program, no clean-up-the-landscape activity, no degree of protection for the wilderness, no antipollution laws can be more than the merest beginning. Of course such measures are worthwhile, but in undertaking them we should acknowledge their superficiality. The devastation of the environment is at bottom a result of the kind of society we have built and the kind of people we are. It follows, therefore, that environmentalists should join forces, wherever common aims can be found, with other groups concerned to change basic institutions. To arrest the deterioration of the environment it will be necessary to control many of the same forces which have prevented us from ending the war in Indochina or giving justice to black Americans. In other words, it will be necessary for ecologists to determine where the destructive power of our society lies and how to cope with it. Knowledge of that kind, needless to say, is political. But then it seems obvious, on reflection, that the study of human ecology will be incomplete until it incorporates a sophisticated mode of political analysis.

Meanwhile, it would be folly, given the character of American institutions, to discount the urgency of our situation either on the ground that technology will provide the solutions or on the ground that countermeasures are proposed. We cannot rely on technology because the essential problem is not technological. It inheres in all of the ways in which this dynamic society generates and uses its power. It calls into question the controlling purposes of all the major institutions which actually determine the nation's impact upon the environment: the great business corporations, the military establishment, the universities, the scientific and technological elites, and the exhilarating expansionary ethos by which we all live. Throughout our brief history, a passion for personal and collective aggrandizement has been the American way. One can only guess at the extent to which forebodings of ecological doom have contributed to the revulsion that so many intelligent young people feel these days for the idea of "success" as a kind of limitless ingestion. In any case, most of the talk about the environmental crisis that turns on the word *pollution,* as if we face a cosmic-scale problem of sanitation, is grossly misleading. What confronts us is an extreme imbalance between society's hunger—the rapidly growing sum of human wants—and the limited capacities of the earth.

nine
ecological
armageddon

ROBERT HEILBRONER

*Robert Heilbroner (b. 1919) is one of the leading
economists to concern himself with the environmental
implications of continued economic growth. Reviewing*
Population, Resources, Environment *(1970) by Paul and
Anne Ehrlich, Heilbroner points out that the environmental
crisis raises fundamental political and social questions,
the recognition and reevaluation of which might offer our
one great hope for ecological salvation. Heilbroner is
the author of* The Limits of American Capitalism *(1967),
and since 1966 he has served on the faculty of the
New School for Social Research.*

Ecology has become the Thing. There are ecological politics,
ecological jokes, ecological bookstores, advertisements,
seminars, teach-ins, buttons. The automobile, symbol of
ecological abuse, has been tried, sentenced to death, and
formally executed in at least two universities (complete with
burial of one victim). Publishing companies are fattening
on books on the sonic boom, poisons in the things we eat,
perils loose in the garden, the dangers of breathing. The
Saturday Review has appended a regular monthly Ecological
Supplement. In short, the ecological issue has assumed the
dimensions of a vast popular fad, for which one can predict
with reasonable assurance the trajectory of all such fads—
a period of intense general involvement, followed by
growing boredom and gradual extinction, save for a
die-hard remnant of the faithful.

This would be a tragedy, for I have slowly become

Source: Robert Heilbroner, "Ecological Armageddon," *New York
Review of Books* 14 (April 23, 1970): 3–4, 6–9. Copyright ©
1970 The New York Review. Reprinted with permission from
The New York Review of Books.

convinced during the last twelve months that the ecological issue is not only of primary and lasting importance, but that it may indeed constitute the most dangerous and difficult challenge that humanity has ever faced. Since these are very large statements, let me attempt to substantiate them by drawing freely on the best single descriptive and analytic treatment of the subject that I have yet seen, *Population, Resources, Environment* by Paul and Anne Ehrlich of Stanford University. Rather than resort to the bothersome procedure of endlessly citing their arguments in quotation marks, I shall take the liberty of reproducing their case in a rather free paraphrase, as if it were my own, until we reach the end of the basic argument, after which I shall make clear some conclusions that I believe lie implicit in their work.

Ultimately, the ecological crisis represents our belated awakening to the fact that we live on what Kenneth Boulding has called, in the perfect phrase, our Spaceship Earth. As in all spaceships, sustained life requires that a meticulous balance be maintained between the capability of the vehicle to support life and the demands made by the inhabitants of the craft. Until quite recently, those demands have been well within the capability of the ship, in its ability both to supply the physical and chemical requirements for continued existence and to absorb the waste products of the voyagers. This is not to say that the earth has been generous—short rations have been the lot of mankind for most of its history—nor is it to deny the recurrent advent of local ecological crises: witness the destruction of whole areas like the erstwhile granaries of North Africa. But famines have passed and there have always been new areas to move to. The idea that the earth as a whole was overtaxed is one that is new to our time.

For it is only in our time that we are reaching the limit of earthly carrying capacity, not on a local but on a global basis. Indeed, as will soon become clear, we are well past that capacity, provided that the level of resource intake and waste output represented by the average American or European is taken as a standard to be achieved by all humanity. To put it bluntly, if we take as the price of a first-class ticket the resource requirements of those passengers who travel in the Northern Hemisphere of the Spaceship, we have now reached a point at which the steerage is condemned to live forever—or at least within the horizon of the technology presently visible—at a second-class level; or a point at which a considerable change in living habits must be imposed on first class if the ship is ever to be converted to a one-class cruise.

This strain on the carrying capacity of the vessel results from the contemporary confluence of three distinct developments, each of which places tremendous or even unmanageable strains on the life-carrying capability of the planet and all of which together simply overload it. The first of these is the enormous strain imposed by the sheer burgeoning of population. The statistics of population growth are by now very well known: the earth's passenger list is growing at a rate that will give us some four billion humans by 1975, and that threatens to give us eight billion by 2010. I say "threatens," since it is likely that the inability of the earth to carry so large a group will result in an actual population somewhat smaller than this, especially in the steerage, where the growth is most rapid and the available resources least plentiful.

We shall return to the population problem later. But meanwhile a second strain is placed on the earth by the simple cumulative effect of *existing* technology (combustion engines, the main industrial processes, present-day agricultural techniques, etc.). This strain is localized mainly in the first-class portions of the vessel where each new arrival on board is rapidly given a standard complement of capital equipment and where the rate of physical and chemical resource transformation per capita steadily mounts. The strain consists of the limited ability of the soil, the water, and the atmosphere of these favored regions to absorb the outpourings of these fast-growing industrial processes.

The most dramatic instance of this limited absorptive power is the rise in the carbon dioxide content of the air due to the steady growth of (largely industrial) combustion. By the year 2000, it seems beyond dispute that the CO_2 content of the air will have doubled, raising the heat-trapping properties of the atmosphere. This so-called greenhouse effect has been predicted to raise mean global temperatures sufficiently to bring catastrophic potential consequences. One possibility is a sequence of climatic changes resulting from a melting of the Arctic ice floes that would result in the advent of a new Ice Age; another is the slumping of the Antarctic ice cap into the sea with a consequent tidal wave that could wipe out a substantial portion of mankind and raise the sea level by 60 to 100 feet.

These are all "iffy" scenarios whose present significance may be limited to alerting us to the immensity of the ecological problem; happily they are of sufficient uncertainty not to cause us immediate worry (it is lucky they are, because it is extremely unlikely that all the massed technological and human energy on earth could arrest such changes once they began). Much closer to home is the burden placed on the earth's carrying capacity by the sheer requirements of a spreading industrial activity for the fuel and mineral resources needed to maintain the going rate of output per person in the first-class cabins. To raise the existing (not the anticipated) population of the earth to American standards would require the annual extraction of 75 times as much iron, 100 times as much copper, 200 times as much lead, and 250 times as much tin as we now take from the earth. Only the known reserves of iron allow us to entertain such fantastic rates of mineral exploitation (and the capital investment needed to bring about such mining operations is in itself staggering to contemplate). All the other requirements exceed by far all known or reasonably anticipated ore reserves. And, to repeat, we have taken into account only today's level of population: to equip the prospective passengers of the year 2010 with this amount of basic raw material would require a doubling of all the above figures.

I will revert later to the consequences of this prospect. First, however, let us pay attention to the third source of overload, this one traceable to the special environment-destroying potential of newly developed technologies. Of these the most important—and if it should ever come to full-scale war, of course the most lethal—is the threat posed by nuclear radiation. I shall not elaborate on this well-known (although not well-believed) danger, pausing to point out only that a nuclear holocaust would in all likelihood exert its principal effect in the Northern Hemisphere. The survivors in the South would be severely hampered in their efforts at reconstruction not only because most of the easily available resources of the world have already been used up, but because most of the technological know-how would have perished along with the populations up North.

But the threats of new technology are by no means limited to the specter of nuclear devastation. There is, immediately at hand, the known devastation of the new chemical pesticides that have now entered more or less irreversibly into the living tissue of the world's population. Most mothers' milk in the United States today—I now quote the Ehrlichs verbatim—"contains so much DDT that it would be declared illegal in interstate commerce if it were sold as cow's milk"; and the DDT intake of infants around the world is twice the daily allowable maximum set by the World Health Organization. We are already, in other words, being exposed to heavy dosages of chemicals whose effects we know to be dangerous, with what ultimate results we shall have to wait nervously to discover. (There is food for thought in the archaeological evidence that one factor in the decline of Rome was the systematic poisoning of upper-class Romans from the lead with which they lined their wine containers.)

But the threat is not limited to pesticides. Barry Commoner predicts an agricultural crisis in the United States within fifty years from the action of our fertilizers, which will either ultimately destroy soil fertility or lead to pollution of the national water supply. At another corner of the new technology, the SST threatens not only to shake us with its boom, but to affect the amount of cloud cover (and climate) by its contrails. And I have not even mentioned the standard pollution problems of smoke, industrial effluents into lakes and rivers, or solid wastes. Suffice it to report that a 1968 UNESCO Conference concluded that man has only about twenty years to go before the planet starts to become uninhabitable because of air pollution alone. Of course "starts to" is imprecise; I am reminded of a cartoon of an industrialist looking at his billowing smokestacks, in front of which a forlorn figure is holding up a placard that says: "We have only 35 years to go." The caption reads, "Boy, that shook me up for a minute. I thought it said 3 to 5 years."

I have left until last the grimmest and gravest threat of all, speaking now on behalf of the steerage. This is the looming inability of the great green earth to bring forth sufficient food to maintain life, even at the miserable threshold of subsistence at which it is now endured by perhaps a third of the world's population. The problem here is the very strong likelihood that population growth will inexorably outpace whatever improvements in fertility and productivity we will be able to apply to the earth's mantle (including the watery fringes of the ocean where sea "farming" is at least technically imaginable). Here the race is basically between two forces: on the one hand, those that give promise that the rate of population increase can be curbed (if not totally halted); and on the other, those that give promise of increasing the amount of sustenance we can wring from the soil.

Both these forces are subtly blended of technological and social factors. Take population growth. The great hope of every ecologist is that an effective birth control technique—cheap, requiring little or no medical supervision, devoid of taboos or religious hindrances—will rapidly and effectively lower the present fertility rates which are doubling world population every thirty-five years

(every twenty-eight years in Africa; every twenty-four in Latin America).
No such device is currently available, although the Pill, the IUD, vasectomies,
abortions, condoms, coitus interruptus, and other known techniques could,
of course, do the job, if the requisite equipment, persuasion (or coercion),
instruction, etc., could be brought to the 80 to 90 percent of the world's people
who know next to nothing about birth control.

It seems a fair conclusion that no such world-wide campaign is apt to be
successful for at least a decade and maybe a generation, although there is always
the hope that a "spontaneous" change in attitudes, similar to that in Hungary
or Japan, will bring about a rapid halt to population growth. But even in
this unlikely event, the sheer "momentum" of population growth still
poses terrible problems. Malcolm Potts, Secretary General of International
Planned Parenthood, has presented a shocking statistical calculation in this
regard: he has pointed out that population growth in India is today adding one
million mouths per month to the Indian subcontinent. If, by some miracle,
fertility rates were to decline tomorrow by 50 percent in India, at the end of
twenty years, owing to the already existing huge numbers of children who would
be moving up into child-bearing ages, population growth in India would still
be taking place at the rate of one million mouths per month.

The other element in the race is our ability to match population growth with
food supplies, at least for a generation or so, while birth control techniques
and campaigns are being perfected. Here the problem is also partly technological,
partly social. The technological part involves the so-called "Green Revolution"
—the development of seeds that are capable, at their best, of improving
yields per acre by a factor of 300 percent, sometimes even more. The problem,
however, is that these new seeds generally require irrigation and fertilizer
to bring their benefits. If India alone were to apply fertilizer at the per capita
level of the Netherlands, she would consume half the world's total output
of fertilizer. This would require a hundredfold expansion of India's present level
of fertilizer use.

Irrigation, the other necessary input for most improved seeds, poses equally
formidable requirements. E. A. Mason of the Oak Ridge National Laboratories
has prepared preliminary estimates of the costs of nuclear-powered "agro-
industrial complexes" in which desalted water and fertilizer would be
produced for use on adjacent farms. It would require twenty-three such plants
per year, each taking care of some three million people, just to keep pace
with present world population growth. Since it would take at least five years to
get these plants into operation, we should begin work today on at least 125
such units. If we assume that no hitches were encountered and that the
technology on paper could be easily translated into a technology *in situ,* the
cost would amount to $315 billion.

There are as well other technical problems of an ecological nature associated
with the Green Revolution—mainly the risk of introducing locally untried
strains of plants that may be subject to epidemic disease. But putting those
difficulties to the side, we must recognize as well the social obstacles that a
successful Green Revolution must overcome. The new seeds can only
be afforded by the upper level of peasantry—not merely because of their cost

(and the cost of the required fertilizer), but because only a rich peasant can take the risk of having the crop turn out badly without himself suffering starvation. Hence the Green Revolution is likely to increase the strains of social stratification within the underdeveloped areas. Then, too, even a successful local crop does not always shed its benefits evenly across a nation, but results all too often in local gluts that cannot be transported to starving areas because of transportation bottlenecks.

None of these discouraging remarks is intended in the slightest to disparage the Green Revolution, which represents the inspired work of dedicated men. But the difficulties must be kept in mind as a corrective to the lulling belief that "science" can easily offset the population boom with larger supplies of food. There is no doubt that supplies of food *can* be substantially increased—rats alone devour some 10–12 percent of India's crop, and insects can ravage up to half of the stored crops of some underdeveloped areas, so that even very "simple" methods of improved storage hold out important prospects of improving basic life-support, quite aside from the longer term hopes of agronomy.

Yet at best these improvements will only stave off the day of reckoning. Ultimately the problem posed by Malthus must be faced—that population tends to increase geometrically, by doubling; and that agriculture does not; so that eventually population *must* face the limit of a food barrier. It is worth repeating the words of Malthus himself in this regard:

Famine seems to be the last, the most dreadful resource of nature. The power of population is so much superior to the power in the earth to produce subsistence for man, that premature death must in some shape or other visit the human race. The vices of mankind are active and able ministers of depopulation. . . . [S]hould they fail in this war of extermination, sickly seasons, epidemics, pestilence, and plague, advance in terrific array, and sweep off their thousands and ten thousands. Should success still be incomplete, gigantic inevitable famine stalks in the rear, and with one mighty blow, levels the population with the food of the world.

This Malthusian prophecy has been so often "refuted," as economists have pointed to the astonishing rates of growth of food output in the advanced nations, that there is a danger of dismissing the warnings of the Ehrlichs as merely another premature alarm. To do so would be a fearful mistake. For unlike Malthus, who assumed that technology would remain constant, the Ehrlichs have made ample allowance for the growth of technological capability, and their approach to the impending catastrophe is not shrill. They merely point out that a mild version of the Malthusian solution is already upon us, for at least half a billion people are chronically hungry or outright starving, and another $1\frac{1}{2}$ billion under or malnourished. Thus we do not have to wait for "gigantic inevitable famine"; it has already come.

What is more important is that the Ehrlichs see the matter in a fundamentally different perspective from Malthus, not as a problem involving supply and demand, but as one involving a total ecological equilibrium. The crisis, as the Ehrlichs see it, is thus both deeper and more complex than merely a shortage of food, although the latter is one of its more horrendous evidences. What threatens the Spaceship Earth is a profound imbalance between the totality of systems by which human life is maintained, and the totality of demands, industrial as well as agricultural, technological as well as demographic, to which that capacity to support life is subjected.

I have no doubt that one can fault bits and pieces of the Ehrlichs' analysis, and there is a note of determined pessimism in their work that leads me to suspect (or at least hope) that there is somewhat more time for adaptation than they suggest. Yet I do not see how their basic conclusion can be denied. Beginning within our lifetimes and rising rapidly to crisis proportions in our children's, humankind faces a challenge comparable to none in its history, with the possible exception of the forced migrations of the Ice Age. It is with the responses to this crisis that I wish to end this essay, for telling and courageous as the Ehrlichs' analysis is, I do not believe that even they have fully faced up to the implications that their own findings present.

The first of these I have already stated: it is the clear conclusion that the underdeveloped countries can *never* hope to achieve parity with the developed countries. Given our present and prospective technology, there are simply not enough resources to permit a "Western" rate of industrial exploitation to be expanded to a population of four billion—much less eight billion—persons. It may well be that most of the population in the underdeveloped world has no ambition to reach Western standards—indeed, does not even know that such a thing as "development" is on the agenda. But the elites of these nations, for all their rhetorical rejection of Western (and especially American) styles of life, do tend to picture a Western standard as the ultimate end of their activities. As it becomes clear that such an objective is impossible, a profound reorientation of views must take place within the underdeveloped nations.

What such a reorientation will be it is impossible to say. For the near future, the outlook for the most population-oppressed areas will be a continuous battle against food shortages, coupled with the permanent impairment of the intelligence of much of the surviving population due to protein deficiencies in childhood. This pressure of population may lead to aggressive searches for *Lebensraum*; or as I have frequently written, may culminate in revolutions of desperation.

In the long run, of course, there is the possibility of considerable growth (although nothing resembling the attainment of a Western standard of consumption). But no quick substantial improvement in their condition seems feasible within the next generation at least. The visions of Sir Charles Snow or the Soviet academician Sakharov for a gigantic transfer of wealth from the rich nations to the poor (20 percent of GNP is proposed) are simply fantasies. Since much of GNP is spatially nontransferable or inappropriate, such a huge levy against GNP would imply shipments of up to 50 percent of much movable output. How this enormous flood of goods would be transported, allocated, absorbed, or maintained—*not to mention relinquished by the donor countries*—is nowhere analyzed by the proponents of such vast aid.

The implications of the ecological crisis for the advanced nations are not any less severe, although they are of a different kind. For it is clear that free industrial growth is just as disastrous for the Western nations as free population growth for those of the East and South. The worship in the West of a growing Gross National Product must be recognized as not only a deceptive but a very dangerous avatar; Kenneth Boulding has begun a campaign, in which I shall join him, to label this statistical monster Gross National Cost.

The necessity to bring our economic activities into a sustainable relationship with the resource capabilities and waste absorption properties of the world will pose two problems for the West. On the simpler level, a whole series of technological problems must be met. Fume-free transportation must be developed on land and air. The cult of disposability must be replaced by that of reusability. Population stability must be attained through tax and other inducements, both to conserve resources and to preserve reasonable population densities. Many of these problems will tax our ingenuity, technical and socio-political, but the main problem they pose is not whether, but *how soon,* they can be solved.

But there is another, deeper question that the developed nations face—at least those that have capitalist economies. This problem can be stated as a crucial test as to who was right—John Stuart Mill or Karl Marx. Mill maintained, in his famous *Principles,* that the terminus of capitalist evolution would be a stationary state, in which the return to capital had fallen to insignificance, and a redistributive tax system would be able to capture any flows of income to the holders of scarce resources, such as land. In effect, he prophesied the transformation of capitalism, in an environment of abundance, into a balanced economy, in which the capitalist, both as the generator of change and as the main claimant on the surplus generated by change, would in effect undergo a painless euthanasia.

The Marxian view is of course quite the opposite. The very essence of capitalism, according to Marx, is expansion—which is to say, the capitalist, as a historical "type," finds his *raison d'être* in the insatiable search for additional money-wealth gained through the constant growth of the economic system. The idea of a "stationary" capitalism is, in Marxian eyes, a contradiction in terms, on a logical par with a democratic aristocracy or an industrial feudalism.

Is the Millian or the Marxian view correct? I do not think that we can yet say. Some economic growth is certainly compatible with a stabilized rate of resource use and disposal, for growth could take the form of the expenditure of additional labor on the improvement (aesthetic or technical) of the national environment. Indeed, insofar as education or cultural activity are forms of national output that require little resource use and result in little waste product, national output could be indefinitely expanded through these and similar activities. But there is no doubt that the main avenue of traditional capitalist accumulation would have to be considerably constrained; that net investment in mining and manufacturing would effectively cease; that the rate and kind of technological change would need to be supervised and probably greatly reduced; and that as a consequence, the flow of profits would almost certainly fall.

Is this imaginable within a capitalist setting—that is, in a nation in which the business ideology permeates the views of nearly all groups and classes, and establishes the bounds of what is possible and natural, and what is not? Ordinarily I do not see how such a question could be answered in any way but negatively, for it is tantamount to asking a dominant class to acquiesce in the elimination of the very activities that sustain it. But this is an extraordinary challenge that may evoke an extraordinary response. Like the challenge posed by war, the ecological crisis affects all classes, and therefore may be sufficient to induce sociological changes that would be unthinkable in ordinary circumstances. The capitalist and managerial classes may see—perhaps even more clearly than the consuming masses—the nature and nearness of the ecological crisis, and may recognize that their only salvation (as human beings, let alone privileged human beings) is an occupational migration into governmental or other posts of power, or they may come to accept a smaller share of the national surplus simply because they recognize that there is no alternative. When the enemy is nature, in other words, rather than another social class, it is at least imaginable that adjustments could be made that would be impossible in ordinary circumstances.

There is, however, one last possibility to which I must also call attention. It is the possibility that the ecological crisis will simply result in the decline or even destruction of Western civilization, and of the hegemony of the scientific-technological view that has achieved so much and cost us so dearly. Great challenges do not always bring great responses, especially when those responses must be sustained over long periods of time and require dramatic changes in life styles and attitudes. Even educated men today are able to deny the reality of the crisis they face: there is wild talk of farming the seas, of transporting men to the planets, of unspecified "miracles" of technology that will avert disaster. Glib as they are, however, at least these suggestions have a certain responsibility when compared to another and much more worrisome response: *Je m'en fiche.* Can we really persuade the citizens of the Western world, who are just now entering the heady atmosphere of a high consumption way of life, that conservation, stability, frugality, and a deep concern for the distant future must now take priority over the personal indulgence for which they have been culturally prepared and which they are about to experience for the first time? Not the least danger of the ecological crisis, as I see it, is that tens and hundreds of millions will shrug their shoulders at the prospects ahead ("What has posterity ever done for us?"), and that the increasingly visible approach of ecological Armageddon will bring not repentance but Saturnalia.

Yet I cannot end this essay on such a note. For it seems to me that the ecological enthusiasts may be right when they speak of the deteriorating environment as providing the *possibility* for a new political rallying ground. If a New Deal, capable of engaging both the efforts and the beliefs of this nation, is the last great hope to which we cling in the face of what seems otherwise to be an inevitable gradual worsening and coarsening of our style of life, it is possible that a determined effort to arrest the ecological decay might prove to be its underlying theme. Such an issue, immediate in the experience of all, carries an appeal that might allow vast improvements to be worked in the American environment, both urban and industrial. I cannot estimate the likelihood of such a political awakening, dependent as these matters are on the dice of personality and the outcome of events at home and abroad. But however slim the possibility of bringing such a change, it does at least make the ecological crisis, unquestionably the gravest long-run threat of our times, potentially the source of its greatest short-term promise.

Let me add a warning that it is not only capitalists who must make an unprecedented ideological adjustment. Socialists must also come to terms with the abandonment of the goal of industrial superabundance on which their vision of a transformed society rests. The stationary equilibrium imposed by the constraints of ecology requires at the very least a reformulation of the kind of economic society toward which socialism sets its course.

ten
the profits
in pollution

RALPH NADER

*Ralph Nader (b. 1934), often termed a consumer advocate,
has become the popular model of the public-service
lawyer. Moving from a Harvard law degree, he published
in 1965 a best-selling exposé of the automobile industry,*
Unsafe at Any Speed. *Since then, he has broadened his
attack on auto safety to a general critique of corporate
irresponsibility in America. In the midst of a growing
corporate enthusiasm for the profits to be realized from
providing a cleaner environment, Nader has taken the
lead in pointing out that, traditionally, industry has been
more the root of the environmental crisis than the
source of its solution.*

The modern corporation's structure, impact, and public
accountability are the central issues in any program designed
to curb or forestall the contamination of air, water, and
soil by industrial activity. While there are other sources of
pollution, such as municipalities dumping untreated or
inadequately treated sewage, industrial processes and
products are the chief contributors to the long-term
destruction of natural resources that each year increases
the risks to human health and safety.

Moreover, through active corporate citizenship, industry
could soon overcome many of the obstacles in the way
of curbing non-corporate pollution. The mighty automobile
industry, centered around and in Detroit, never thought
it part of its role to press the city of Detroit to construct a
modern sewage treatment plant. The automobile moguls,
whose products, according to Department of Health,

Source: Appeared originally in a slightly different form as
"Corporations and Pollution," *The Progressive* 34 (April 1970):
19–22. Reprinted by permission of the author.

Education and Welfare data, account for fifty-five to sixty per cent of the nation's air pollution, remained silent as the city's obsolete and inadequate sewage facilities dumped the wastes of millions into the Detroit River. Obviously, local boosterism does not include such elementary acts of corporate citizenship.

The toilet training of industry to keep it from further rupturing the ecosystem requires an overhaul of the internal and external levers which control corporations. There are eight areas in which policies must be changed to create the pressures needed to make corporate entities and the people who run them cease their destruction of the environment:

ONE—The conventional way of giving the public a share in private decisions that involve health and safety hazards is to establish mandatory standards through a public agency. But pollution control standards set by governmental agencies can fall far short of their purported objectives unless they are adequately drafted, kept up to date, vigorously enforced, and supported by sanctions when violated. Behind the adoption of such standards, there is a long administrative process, tied to a political infrastructure. The scientific-engineering-legal community has a key independent role to play in this vital and complex administrative-political process. Almost invariably, however, its talents have been retained on behalf of those to be regulated. Whether in Washington or in state capitals around the country, the experts demonstrate greater loyalty to their employers than to their professional commitments in the public interest.

This has been the regular practice of specialists testifying in behalf of coal and uranium mining companies on the latter's environmental contamination in Appalachia and the Rocky Mountain regions. Perhaps the most egregious example of willing corporate servility was a paper entitled "We've Done the Job—What's Next?" delivered by Charles M. Heinen, Chrysler's vehicle emissions specialist, at a meeting of the Society of Automotive Engineers last spring.

Heinen, whose paper bordered on technical pornography, said the auto industry had solved the vehicle pollution problem with an eighty per cent reduction of hydrocarbons and a seventy per cent reduction of carbon monoxide between the 1960 and 1970 model years. He avoided mentioning at least four other vehicle pollutants—nitrogen oxides, lead, asbestos, and rubber tire pollutants. He also failed to point out that the emissions control performance of new cars degrades after a few thousand miles, and that even when new they do not perform under traffic conditions as they do when finely tuned at a company test facility. The overall aggregate pollution from ever greater numbers of vehicles in more congested traffic patterns also escaped Heinen's company-indentured perceptions.

TWO—Sanctions against polluters are feeble and out of date, and, in any case, are rarely invoked. For example, the Federal air quality act has no criminal penalties no matter how willful and enduring the violations. In New Jersey, New York, and Illinois, a seventy-one year old Federal anti-water pollution law was violated with total impunity by industry until the Justice Department moved against a few of the violators in recent months. Other violators in other states are yet to be subjected to the law's enforcement. To be effective, sanctions should come in various forms, such as non-reimbursable fines, suspensions, dechartering of corporations, required disclosure of violations in company promotional materials, and more severe criminal penalties. Sanctions, consequently, should be tailored to the seriousness and duration of the violation.

It is expressive of the anemic and nondeterrent quality of existing sanctions that offshore oil leaks contaminating beaches for months, as in Santa Barbara, brought no penalty to any official of any offending company. The major controversy in Santa Barbara was whether the company—Union Oil—or the Government or the residents would bear the costs of cleaning up the mess. And even if the company bore the costs initially, the tax laws would permit a considerable shifting of this cost onto the general taxpayer.

THREE—The existing requirements for disclosure of the extent of corporate pollution are weak and flagrantly flouted. The Federal Water Pollution Control Administration (FWPCA) has been blocked since 1963 by industrial polluters (working with the Federal Bureau of the Budget) from obtaining information from these companies concerning the extent and location of discharges of pollutants into the nation's waterways. For three years, the National Industrial Waste Inventory has been held up by the Budget Bureau and its industry "advisers," who have a decisive policy role. Led by the steel, paper, and petroleum industries, corporate polluters have prevented the FWPCA from collecting specific information on what each company is putting into the water. Such information is of crucial importance to the effective administration of the water pollution law and the allocation of legal responsibility for violations.

Counties in California have been concealing from their citizens the identity of polluters and the amounts of pollution, using such weak, incredible arguments to support their cover-up as the companies' fear of revealing "trade secrets." California state agencies have refused to disclose pesticide application data to representatives of orchard workers being gradually poisoned by the chemicals. Once again the trade secret rationale was employed.

The real reason for secrecy is that disclosure of such information would raise public questions about why government agencies have not been doing their jobs—and would facilitate legal action by injured persons against the polluters. What must be made clear to both corporate and public officials is that no one has the right to a trade secret in lethality.

Massive and meticulous "fish bowl" disclosure requirements are imperative if citizens are to be alerted, at the earliest possible moment, to the flow of silent violence assaulting their health and safety, and that of unborn generations as well. This disclosure pattern, once established, must not lapse into a conspiracy between private and public officials, a conspiracy of silence against citizens and the public interest. A good place to start with such company-by-company disclosure is in the corporation's annual report, which now reveals only financial profits or losses; it should also reveal the social costs of pollution by composition and tonnage.

FOUR—Corporate investment in research and development of pollution controls

is no longer a luxury to be left to the decision or initiative of a few company
officers. Rather, such research and development must be required by law to
include reinvestment of profits, the amount depending on the volume of
pollution inflicted on the public. For example, in 1969 General Motors grossed
$24 billion, yet last year spent less than $15 million on vehicle and plant
pollution research and development, although its products and plants
contribute some thirty-five per cent of the nation's air pollution by tonnage. A
formula proportional to the size of a company and its pollution could be devised
as law, with required periodic reporting of the progress of the company's
research and its uses. A parallel governmental research and development
program aimed at developing pollution-free product prototypes suitable for mass
production, and a Federal procurement policy favoring the purchase of
less-polluting products, are essential external impacts.

FIVE—Attention must be paid to the internal climate for free expression and
due process within the corporate structure. Again and again, the internal
discipline of the corporate autocracy represses the civic and professional spirit of
employees who have every right to speak out or blow the whistle on their
company after they have tried in vain, working from the inside, to bring about
changes that will end pollution practices. Professional employees—scientists,
engineers, physicians—have fewer due process safeguards than the blue collar
workers in the same company protected by their union contract.

When Edward Gregory, a Fisher Body plant inspector for General Motors in
St. Louis, publicly spoke out in 1966 on inadequate welding that exposed
Chevrolet passengers to exhaust leakage, the company ignored him for a few
years, but eventually recalled more than two million cars for correction.
GM knew better than to fire Gregory, a member of the United Auto Workers.

In contrast, scientists and engineers employed by corporations privately tell me
of their reluctance to speak out—within their companies or outside them—
about hazardous products. This explains why the technical elites are rarely in the
vanguard of public concern over corporate contamination. Demotion, ostracism,
dismissal, are some of the corporate sanctions against which there is little
or no recourse by the professional employee. A new corporate constitutionalism
is needed, guaranteeing employees' due process rights against arbitrary
reprisals, but its precise forms require the collection of data and extensive
study. Here is a major challenge to which college faculty and students can
respond on the campus and in field work.

SIX—The corporate shareholder can act, as he rarely does, as a prod and lever
for jolting corporate leaders out of their lethargy. The law and the lawyers have
rigged the legal system to muffle the voice of shareholders, particularly those
concerned with the broader social costs of corporate enterprise. However,
for socially conscious and determined stockholders there are many functions that
can be performed to help protect the public (including themselves) from
industrial pollution.

Shareholders must learn to take full advantage of such corporate practices as
cumulative voting, which permits the "single-shot" casting of all of a

shareholder's ballots for one member of the board of directors. Delegations of stockholders can give visibility to the issues by lobbying against their company's ill-advised policies in many forums apart from the annual meeting—legislative hearings, agency proceedings, town meetings, and the news media, for example. These delegations will be in a position to expose company officers to public judgment, something from which executives now seem so insulated in their daily corporate activities.

SEVEN—Natural, though perhaps unexercised, countervailing forces in the private sector can be highly influential incentives for change. For example, the United Auto Workers have announced that pollution will be an issue in the collective bargaining process with automobile company management this year; the union hopes to secure for workers the right not to work in polluting activities, or in a polluted environment. Insurance companies could become advocates for loss prevention in the environmental field when confronted with policyholder, shareholder, and citizen demonstrative action. Through their political influence, their rating function in evaluating risks and setting premium charges, and their research and development capability, insurance companies could exert a key countervailing stress on polluters. Whether they do or not will first depend on citizen groups to whip them into action.

EIGHT—Environmental lawsuits, long blocked by a conservative judiciary and an inflexible judicial system, now seem to be coming into their own—a classic example of how heightened public expectations, demands, and the availability of facts shape broader applications of ancient legal principles. Environmental pollution is environmental violence—to human beings and to property. The common law has long recognized such violence against the person as actionable or enjoinable. What has been lacking is sufficient evidence of harm and avoidability to persuade judges that such hitherto invisible long-range harm outweighed the economic benefits of the particular plant activity in the community.

It now appears that such lawsuits will gain greater acceptance, especially as more evidence and more willing lawyers combine to breathe contemporary reality into long-standing legal principles. An amendment to the U.S. Constitution providing citizens with basic rights to a clean environment has been proposed; similar amendments to state constitutions are being offered. Such generic provisions can only further the judicial acceptance of environmental lawsuits. Imaginative and bold legal advocacy is needed here. The *forced consumption* of industrial pollutants by 200 million Americans must lead to a recognition of legal rights in environmental control such as that which developed with civil rights for racial minorities over the last two decades.

Three additional points deserve the attention of concerned citizens:

First, a major corporate strategy in combating anti-pollution measures is to engage workers on the company side by leading them to believe that such measures would threaten their livelihood. This kind of industrial extortion in a community—especially a company town—has worked before and will again unless citizens anticipate and confront it squarely.

Second, both industry spokesmen and their governmental allies (such as the President's Science Adviser, Lee DuBridge) insist that consumers will have to pay the price of pollution control. While this point of view may be an unintended manifestation of the economy's administered price structure, it cannot go unchallenged. Pollution control must not become another lever to lift up excess profits and fuel the fires of inflation. The costs of pollution control technology should come from corporate profits which have been enhanced by the use of the public's environment as industry's private sewer. The sooner industry realizes that it must bear the costs of cleanups, the more likely it will be to employ the quickest and most efficient techniques.

Finally, those who believe deeply in a humane ecology must act in accordance with their beliefs. They must so order their consumption and disposal habits that they can, in good conscience, preach what they actually practice. In brief, they must exercise a personal discipline as they advocate the discipline of governments and corporations.

The battle of the environmentalists is to preserve the physiological integrity of people by preserving the natural integrity of land, air, and water. The planet earth is a seamless structure with a thin slice of sustaining air, water, and soil that supports almost four billion people. This thin slice belongs to all of us, and we use it and hold it in trust for future earthlings. Here we must take our stand.

eleven
the eco-establishment

KATHERINE BARKLEY AND STEVE WEISSMAN

*Katherine Barkley and Steve Weissman are both affiliated
with the Pacific Studies Center at Palo Alto, California,
a research collective that studies the social, political, and
economic nature and impact of American capitalism at
home and abroad. Their description of the "Eco-
Establishment" is an amalgam of the old tradition of
muckraking journalism and the newer spirit of radical
research. In tracing the environmental crusade back
to the Rockefeller interests rather than to Rachel Carson,
they follow more in the tradition of Samuel Hays
than Leonard Bates.*

Ask Vietnam protesters about the April 22 National
Environmental Teach-In and they'll tell you it's a scheme
to contain their spring offensive against the ecological
disaster in Southeast Asia. Ask young blacks about this new
movement to save the ecosystem and they'll tell you that it
is a way of distracting attention from the old movement
that was supposed to save their skins.

   Then go and talk to an environmental activist, a Survival
Walker. Ask him why the ecology movement has turned
its back on Vietnam and civil rights and he'll explain,
with a convincing freshness the old New Left has lost,
that the sky is falling. He'll point out that we all have to
breathe and that none of us—white or black, Vietnamese
peasant or American marine—has much of a future on CO_2.
We all must eat, and a diet of pesticides is deadly.
We all need water, and the dwindling supplies are unfit
for human (or even industrial) consumption. We all
depend on the same limited forests, mines, oceans and soil,
and we are all going to choke on the same waste and
pollution.

Source: Katherine Barkley and Steve Weissman, "The Eco-
Establishment," *Ramparts* 8 (May 1970): 48–49, 54, 56, 58.
Reprinted by permission of the publisher.

To this new ecology activist, nothing could be more obvious: we've all got to unite behind the overriding goal of unfouling our common nest before it's too late, turning back the pages of the environmental doomsday book. If we succeed, then we can get back to these other questions. There is no stopping, he will add, an idea whose time has come.

He will be right, too—though a bit naive about where ideas come from and where movements go. Environment *will be* the issue of the '70's, but not simply because the air got thicker or the oceans less bubbly, or even because the war in Vietnam got too bloody to have to think about every day. It will be the issue of the '70's because such stewards of the nation's wealth as the Ford Foundation, with its Resources for the Future, Inc. (RFF), and Laurance Rockefeller's Conservation Foundation needed a grass-roots movement to help consolidate their control over national policymaking, bolster their hold over world resources, and escalate further cycles of useless economic growth.

II

The environment bandwagon is not as recent a phenomenon as it seems. It began to gather momentum back in the mid-'60's under the leadership of Resources for the Future. "The relationship of people to resources, which usually has been expressed in terms of quantity, needs to be restated for modern times to emphasize what is happening to the quality of resources," warned RFF President Joseph L. Fisher in his group's 1964 report. "The wide variety of threats to the quality of the environment may well embrace the gravest U.S. resources problem for the next generation." The following year, Resources for the Future established a special research and educational program in environmental quality, funded with a $1.1 million grant from its parent organization, the Ford Foundation.

Created by Ford in the early '50's during the scare over soaring materials costs, RFF had just made its name in conservation by organizing the Mid-Century Conference on Resources for the Future, the first major national conservation conference since Teddy Roosevelt and Gifford Pinchot staged the National Governors' Conference in 1908. Held in 1953, the Mid-Century Conference mustered broad support from both the country's resource users and conservers for the national conservation policy already spelled out by President Truman's Materials Policy Commission. It was this Commission, headed by William S. Paley (board chairman of CBS and a founding director of RFF), which had openly affirmed the nation's inalienable right to extract cheap supplies of raw materials from the underdeveloped countries, and which set the background for Eisenhower and Dulles' oft-quoted concern over the fate of the tin and tungsten of Southeast Asia. Insuring adequate supplies of resources for the future became a conservationist byword.

By the mid-'60's, Resources for the Future had begun to broaden its concern to include resource quality, thus setting the tone for a decade of conservationist rhetoric and behavior. The trustees of the Ford Foundation, an executive committee of such international resource users and polluters as Esso and Ford Motor, established a separate Resources and Environment Division which, since 1966, has nourished such groups as Open Space Action Committee, Save-the-Redwoods League, Massachusetts Audubon Society, Nature Conservancy, and the Environmental Defense Fund. A year later, the Rockefeller Foundation set up an Environmental Studies Division, channeling money to the National Academy of Science and RFF and to Laurance Rockefeller's own pet project, the Conservation Foundation.

The conservationist-planners' new concern over threats to the quality of resources, and to life itself, was actually an outgrowth of their earlier success in assuring cheap and plentiful raw materials. It had become clear that supplies of resources would be less a problem than the immense amount of waste generated as a by-product of those now being refined. The more industry consumed, the more it produced and sold, the larger and more widespread the garbage dumps. Rivers and lakes required costly treatment to make water suitable for use in homes and industry. Smoggy air corroded machines, ruined timberlands, reduced the productivity of crop lands and livestock—to say nothing of its effect on the work capacity of the average man. Pesticides were killing more than pests, and raising the spectre of cumulative disaster. Cities were getting noisier, dirtier, uglier and more tightly packed, forcing the middle class to the suburbs and the big urban landowners to the wall. "Ugliness," Lyndon Johnson exclaimed sententiously, "is costly."

This had long been obvious to the conservationists. Something had to be done, and the elite resource planners took as their model for action the vintage 1910 American conservation movement, especially its emphasis on big business cooperation with big government.

III

When the 1890 census officially validated the fact that the frontier was closed, a generation of business and government leaders realized with a start that the American Eden had its bounds. Land, timber and water were all limited, as was the potential for conflicts over their apportionment. What resources should timbermen, grazers or farmers exploit? What should be preserved as a memory of the American past? Who would decide these questions? The conservationists—Teddy Roosevelt, Chief Forester Gifford Pinchot and some of the bigger timber, grazing and agricultural interests—pushed heavily for a new policy to replace the crude and wanton pillage which had been part of the frontier spirit. While preservationists like John Muir were fighting bitterly against any and all use of wild areas by private interests, the conservationists wanted only to make sure that the environment would be exploited with taste and efficiency.

Roosevelt and his backers won out, of course. And the strategy they used is instructive: failing initially to muster congressional support for their plan, they mobilized a broadly based conservation movement, supposedly to regulate the private interests which they in fact represented. Backed by the widespread public support it had whipped up, the conservationist juggernaut then began to move the country toward a more regulated—but still private—exploitation of its riches.

Of course, the private interests which had helped draft this policy also moved—to staff the regulatory agencies, provide jobs for retiring regulators, and generally to put the right man in the right niche most of the time. Within short order, the regulatory agencies were captives of the interests they were supposed to regulate, and they were soon being used as a screen which kept the public from seeing the way that small interests were squeezed out of the competition for resources. Their monopoly position thus strengthened by regulatory agencies, these large interests found it easy to pass the actual costs of regulation on to the citizen consumer.

IV

The old American conservation movement had reacted out of fear over resource scarcities; the new movement of the mid-'60's feared, as well, the destruction of resource quality. And the corporation conservationists and their professional planners in organizations like Resources for the Future once again looked to government regulations as an answer to the difficulties they foresaw. Only this time the stakes were much higher than they had been at the early part of the century. Many of the resource planners want an all-encompassing environmental agency or Cabinet level Department of Resources, Environment and Population. Holding enormous power over a wide range of decisions, this coordinating apparatus would be far more convenient for the elite than the present array of agencies, each influenced by its own interest groups.

Who will benefit from this increased environmental consciousness and who will pay is already quite clear to business, if not to most young ecology activists. "The elite of business leadership," reports Fortune, "strongly desire the federal government to step in, set the standards, regulate all activities pertaining to the environment, and help finance the job with tax incentives." The congressional background paper for the 1968 hearings on National Policy on Environmental Quality, prepared with the help of Rockefeller's Conservation Foundation, spells out the logic in greater detail: "Lack of national policy for the environment has now become as expensive to the business community as to the Nation at large. In most enterprises, a social cost can be carried without undue burden if all competitors carry it alike. For example, industrial waste disposal costs can, like other costs of production, be reflected in prices to consumers. But this becomes feasible only when public law and administration put all comparable forms of waste-producing enterprises under the same requirements." Only the truly powerful could be so candid about their intention to pick the pocket of the consumer to pay for the additional costs they will be faced with.

The resource planners are also quite frank about the wave of subsidies they expect out of the big clean-up campaign. "There will have to be a will to provide funds," explains Joseph Fisher, "to train the specialists, do the research and experimentation, build the laws and institutions through which more rapid progress [in pollution control] can be made, and of course, build the facilities and equipment." The coming boondoggles—replete with tax incentives, direct government grants, and new products—will make the oil

depletion allowance seem tame. And what's more, it will be packaged as
a critical social service.

The big business conservationists will doubtless be equally vocal about the
need for new bond issues for local water and sewage treatment facilities; lead
crusades to overcome reluctance of the average citizen to vote "yes" on bond
measures; and then, as bondholders themselves, skim a nice tax-free six or seven
per cent off the top.

It isn't just the citizen and taxpayer who will bear the burden, however.
Bedraggled Mother Nature, too, will pay. Like the original conservation
movement it is emulating, today's big business conservation is not interested in
preserving the earth; it is rationally reorganizing for a more efficient rape
of resources (e.g., the export of chemical-intensive agribusiness) and the
production of an ever grosser national product.

The seeming contradictions are mind-boggling: industry is combatting waste
so it can afford to waste more; it is planning to produce more (smog-controlled)
private autos to crowd more highways, which means even more advertising
to create more "needs" to be met by planned obsolescence. Socially, the result
is disastrous. Ecologically, it could be the end.

Why don't the businessmen simply stop their silly growthmanship? They
can't. If one producer slowed down in the mad race, he'd be eaten up by his
competitors. If all conspired together to restrain growth permanently, the
unemployment and cutbacks would make today's recession look like full
employment, and the resulting unrest would make today's dissent look like play
time at Summerhill.

V

They began in the mid-'60's in low key, mobilizing the academicians, sprinkling
grants and fellowships at the "better" schools, and coordinating research
efforts of Resources for the Future, the Conservation Foundation, RAND,
Brookings Institution, the National Academy of Science and the Smithsonian
Institution. Major forums were held in 1965 and 1966 on "The Quality of the
Environment" and "Future Environments of North America." Research
findings were programmed directly into industrial trade associations and business
firms.

Then the resource people put their men and programs in the official
spotlight: Laurance Rockefeller (founder of and major donor to the Conservation
Foundation and also a director of RFF) chaired both the White House
Conference on Natural Beauty and the Citizens' Advisory Committee on
Recreation and Natural Beauty (which Nixon has rechristened his Citizens'
Advisory Committee on Environmental Quality). Conservation Foundation
President Russell Train headed up Nixon's Task Force on Resources and
Environment, with help from Fisher and several other directors of RFF and the
Conservation Foundation, and then became Undersecretary of Interior.

Then the media were plugged in, an easy task for men who have in their
hands the direction of CBS, National Educational Television, Time-Life-Fortune,
Christian Science Monitor, New York Times and Cowles publications, as well

as many of the trade journals and conservation magazines. Independent media, seeing that environment was now news, picked up and broadcast the studies which the conservation elite had produced. Public opinion leaders told their public, in Business Week's words, "to prepare for the approval of heavy public and private spending to fight pollution."

Finally, the grass roots were given the word. RFF, Ford and Rockefeller had long worked with and financed the old-time conservation groups, from Massachusetts Audubon to the Sierra Club, and now the big money moved beyond an appreciation of wilderness to a greater activism. When, for example, David Brower broke with the Sierra Club, it was Robert O. Anderson of Atlantic-Richfield and RFF who gave him $200,000 to set up Friends of the Earth (prudently channeling the donation through the organization's tax-exempt affiliate, the John Muir Institute).

When Senator Gaylord Nelson and Congressman Pete McCloskey got around to pushing the National Teach-In, it was the Conservation Foundation, the Audubon Society and the American Conservation Association which doled out the money while Friends of the Earth was putting together *The Environmental Handbook,* meant to be the Bible of the new movement.

The big business conservationists and their professionals didn't buy off the movement; they built it.

VI

Ecology activists out picketing a polluter or cleaning up a creek will have total freedom to make up their own minds about the threats to our environment, and they will have every right to choose their own course of constructive action. Yet they will surely never get a dime from Robert Anderson, or even a farthing from Ford or Rockefeller. And so far, the grass-roots ecology movement has done nothing but echo the eco-elite.

Ecology, unlike most of the fractured scientific field, is holistic. It talks of life and its environment as a totality: how organisms relate to each other and to the system which provides their life-support system. As a discipline applied to human affairs, then, ecology should help us get a whole view of our natural and social environment—from oxygen cycles to business cycles, from the jeopardized natural environment to the powerful institutional environment which creates that jeopardy. If it revealed these interconnections, ecology would become, as it has been called, a "subversive science," subverting the polluters and resource-snatchers who now control the conservation of the nation's wealth. It would point the finger not simply at profit-making polluters or greedy consumers, but at the great garbage-creation system itself—the corporate capitalist economy.

But this is a far cry from the ecology movement as we have inherited it. Ecology, the science of interconnections, becomes a matter of cleaning up beaches and trying to change individuals' habits and attitudes, while ignoring the institutions which created them and practically all environmental damage.

The grass-roots ecology groups do have politics—the politics of consumer boycotts, shareholder democracy and interest group pluralism, all of which show a wonderfully anachronistic faith in the fairness of the market, political and economic. "If Dow pollutes," say the boycotters, "then we just won't buy Saran Wrap." If Super Suds won't make biodegradable soap, we'll buy Ivory. If Ford and Chevy won't make steam cars, we'll buy Japanese imports. From the planned obsolescence in automobiles, to 20 brands of toothpaste, much of what industry produces is insulting to the intelligence while also serving no real need; it is waste, to say nothing of the enormous pollution entailed in overproduction.

Consumer sovereignty has gone the way of the dodo, its passing noted two decades back by that stalwart defender of the new corporate capitalism, John Kenneth Galbraith. Consumers just don't control what gets produced, or how. To educate or build support for some stronger action, boycotts, like the picket line, work well. But to change production habits, an ecology movement will really have to pull the big plug at the other end of the TV transmitter, or better, at the production line itself.

Failing in the economic arena, the ecology groups can of course try their hand directly in the political marketplace. Oil has its lobby, the auto manufacturers theirs. Why not a People's Lobby? Californians have already created one, which is now pushing in Sacramento for a referendum "to make the polluters pay." The Environmental Defense League, geared primarily to the court system, is also defending the environment in Congress. The Sierra Club has already lost its tax-exempt status for being too political, and a number of the older conservation groups are pushing new, streamlined legislation. The strategy seems to be paying off, winning victories here and there. Most of the victories, however, merely strengthen the regulatory agencies, which, after public vigilance peters out, will become tools of the big corporations.

Where boycotts and stockholder strategies simply fail, the interest group politics may lead the ecology movement off the edge of a very well conserved cliff. Eco-catastrophe threatens to kill us all—and Mother Nature, too. But to engage in the give-and-take of interest group politics, the ecologists must grant serious consideration to and must compromise with the oil interests, auto manufacturers and other powerful business groups. Standard Oil gets Indonesia only if they will market that country's prized sulphur-free oil here; the auto makers can keep producing their one-man-one-car civilization in return for making additional profit (and apparent compromise) on smog control. The world is dying: write your congressman today.

From lobbying, the eco-groups will move into the nearest election, trying to put Paul Ehrlich or David Brower in office. But elections aren't won on single issues. Allies must be wooed, coalitions built. Already parochial and out of sympathy with the blacks and other out-groups, the environmentalists, anxious to infiltrate the electoral system, will become even more respectable and more careful to avoid contamination by "extreme" positions or people. They will become further compartmentalized and will be at dead center, sacrificing even those of their own who refuse to compromise.

Avoiding "politics," the ecologists have taken up the old liberal shuck. Give equal freedom to aristocrats and the people, to bosses and workers, to landlords and tenants, and let both sides win. The scheme, of course, overlooks the one-sided distribution of resources, money and media-power. Some "reformers" will have all they need, but their solution, which will become *the* solution, is itself a good part of the problem. Profit-seekers and growth-mongers can't co-exist with Mother Nature and her fragile children without doing them irreparable harm.

To save any semblance of democracy, a decent relationship to the environment and perhaps the environment itself—ecology, the "in" movement, must become a movement of the outs. It must be committed to a long-term militant fight on more clearly understood grounds—its *own* grounds. That too might be impossible. But, as Eugene V. Debs once observed, it's a lot better to fight for what you want and not get it, than to fight for—and get—what you don't want.

twelve
black
ecology

NATHAN HARE

*The black scholar Nathan Hare (b. 1934) believes that if
the movement for environmental preservation is to
achieve the larger results hoped for by its supporters,
it will have to come to grips with the problem of
institutional racism in America. He reminds us that the
question of environment is related to the oldest and most
basic of American problems, that of race, and that the
imperative need for social justice must be honored before a
satisfactory solution to either can be found. Hare holds
a doctorate in sociology from the University of Chicago
and served on the faculty at Howard University in
Washington, D.C. from 1961 to 1967. He is the author of*
The Black Anglo Saxons *and the editor and founder
of the journal,* The Black Scholar.

The emergence of the concept of ecology in American life
is potentially of momentous relevance to the ultimate
liberation of black people. Yet blacks and their environmental interests have been so blatantly omitted that blacks
and the ecology movement currently stand in contradiction
to each other.

   The legitimacy of the concept of black ecology accrues
from the fact that: (1) the black and white environments
not only differ in degree but in nature as well; (2) the
causes and solutions to ecological problems are fundamentally different in the suburbs and ghetto (both of
which human ecologists regard as "natural [or ecological]
areas)"; and (3) the solutions set forth for the "ecological
crisis" are reformist and evasive of the social and political
revolution which black environmental correction demands.

Source: Nathan Hare, "Black Ecology," *The Black Scholar*
1 (April 1970): 2–8. Reprinted by permission of The Black Scholar.

In the realm of white ecology, pollution "closes your beaches and prevents your youngsters from wading, swimming, boating, water-skiing, fishing, and other recreation close to home." And, "we want clear water, for boating, and swimming, and fishing—and clean water just to look at."

Similar involvement includes the planting of redwood trees, saving the American eagle, and redeeming terrestrial beauty. Thus it is seen that ecologists aimed at the hearts and purse strings of industrialists and hit the eyeballs of the white bourgeoisie.

Ecology accordingly has come to refer for the most part to chemical and physical or esthetic conditions only, while professional ecologists themselves have been known to differ in their definition of ecology.

> . . . the concept is borrowed from biology, where it means the study of relations between organisms and environment. In biological usage it includes relations between individual organisms and environment (autecology) and between groups and environment (synecology). In social science it is restricted to human synecology, that is, the study of relations between human groups (or populations) and their respective environments, especially their physical environments.

A recent U.S. Department of Health, Education and Welfare report defines environment as "the aggregate of all the external conditions and influences affecting the life and development of an organism, human behavior, society, etc." It is imperative therefore for us to understand how both the physical and social environments of blacks and whites have increasingly evolved as contrasts.

With the industrialization and urbanization of American society, there arose a relatively more rapid and drastic shift of blacks from Southern farms to Northern factories, particularly during periods when they were needed in war industries. Moreover, urban blacks have been increasingly imprisoned in the physical and social decay in the hearts of major central cities, an imprisonment which most emphatically seems doomed to continue. At the same time whites have fled to the suburbs and the exurbs, separating more and more the black and white worlds. The "ecology crisis" arose when the white bourgeoisie, who have seemed to regard the presence of blacks as a kind of pollution, discovered that a sample of what they and their rulers had done to the ghetto would follow them to the suburb.

But there is a greater degree of all varieties of pollutants in the black ghetto, which also lies extremely exposed to the most final variety of environmental destruction imaginable—the "sneak atom bomb attack peril" this month reported by an authoritative study made by Great Britain's Institute for Strategic Studies.

> Say Russia does drop a 10-megaton bomb on Washington, D.C., or Chicago, for example. Up to five miles from ground zero (the point of the explosion), nine out of ten of all inhabitants would be killed

instantly and the rest seriously injured or victimized by radiation.
All structures would be demolished. From 5 to 9.7 miles out, half of
the inhabitants would be killed, a third of them injured, all others
dazed, shocked, and sickened by radiation, and all buildings damaged
beyond repair. . . . In other words, this would just about take care
of the Negro community.

But the ecological ordeal of the black race does not have to wait for a nuclear attack; present conditions are deadly enough. The environmental crisis of whites (in both its physical and social aspects) already pales in comparison to that of blacks.

In addition to a harsher degree of industrial pollutants such as "smoke, soot, dust, fly ash, fumes, gases, stench, and carbon monoxide"—which, as in the black ghetto, "if there is no wind or if breezes are blocked dispersal will not be adequate"—the black ghetto contains a heavier preponderance or ratio, for instance, of rats and cockroaches. These creatures comprise an annoyance and "carry filth on their legs and bodies and may spread disease by polluting food. They destroy food and damage fabrics and bookbindings." Blacks also are more exposed to accidents, the number four killer overall and number one in terms of working years lost by a community.

. . . poverty amid affluence, urban squalor and decay, and alienation
of young people pollute the environment as much as garbage and
industrial smoke. . . . A polluted political system which enables a
handful of senile Southerners to dominate, through the seniority system,
the law making body of a supposedly free people is a political system
which finds racism, poverty, and poisoned rivers equally congenial in
its scheme of things.

Moreover, "the ecological perspective directs attention to various kinds of phenomena. These include, among others: (1) the psychological behavior of persons (singly and in groups of various kinds) . . ." Crime, insanity and other forms of social pathology pollute the central city environment.

It would be a tragic mistake to consider only the material costs of
slums. The great expansion of slums in recent times has become a most
serious social problem because the areas demoralize a large segment
of the urban population.

At the heart of this predicament, though not that alone, is the crowded conditions under which most black persons must live. Black spatial location and distribution not only expose blacks to more devastating and divergent environmental handicaps; they also affect black social and psychological adjustment in a number of subtle ways.

At certain levels of optimum density, flies in fruit jars have been known to die in droves and rats in crowded places to attack and eat their young and

otherwise behave in strange and aberrant ways. Frantz Fanon and others have
patiently charted the way in which oppressed people so crowded turn upon
themselves when, for whatever reason, they feel too weak to fight their
oppressor. Blacks accordingly are relatively more prone to be victims, contrary
to popular belief, of all major crimes of violence as well as a number of other
forms. Although it is true that blacks also exhibit higher rates of criminal
activity, this merely stands in ecological succession to such groups as the Irish
and Italians who in other eras inhabited the lower strata of the urban slums.
Only a minority of blacks are criminals; more are victims of crime. Due largely
to existence in a criminally infested environment, blacks are about four times as
likely to fall victim to forcible rape and robbery and about twice as likely to face
burglary and aggravated assault.

The social and psychological consequences of overcrowding are tangled and
myriad in degree. To begin with, the more persons per unit of space the less
important each individual there; also the noisier the place, other things equal,
and the greater the probability of interpersonal conflict. Studies show that there
is a greater hearing loss with age and that much of it is due to honking horns,
loud engines and general traffic noise. The importance of space to contentment
also is suggested by the fact that in a survey of reasons for moving to the urban
fringe, that of "less congested, more room" was twenty times more frequently
given than the fact that the environment was "cleaner."

The extent of black overcrowding may be seen in the fact that if population
density were as great for the United States at large as it is for some blocks
in Harlem, every person in the nation could live in one-half of New York City.
Using the yardstick of 1.5 persons per room, blacks are about four times as
likely to be overcrowded as whites and they also are more often impelled to live
"doubled up" with another family. This necessity for doubling up imposes
physical and psychological stress and affects self-perception and social behavior.
A study of working class blacks in Chicago revealed that most of them, owing to
a lack of space for beds, slept less than five hours in a given night.

But the residential pollution of blacks rests not alone in overcrowding and
the greater prevalence of unsightly and unsanitary debris and commercial units
such as factories. The very housing afforded blacks is polluted. This fact is
crucial when we consider that the word "ecology" was derived by a German
biologist from the word "aikos" meaning "house." A house, like the clothes we
wear, is an extension of one's self. It may affect "privacy, child-rearing practices,
and housekeeping or study habits." Three of every ten dwellings inhabited by
black families are dilapidated or without hot water, toilet or bath. Many more
are clearly fire hazards.

The shortage of adequate housing and money for rent produces high rates of
black mobility which have far-reaching effects on the black social environment.
It means that blacks will disproportionately live among strangers for longer
periods of time and, in the case of children, attend school in strange classrooms.

The household and neighborhood environments of blacks are perhaps of
greater detriment to black health. The ability to control temperature and

humidity at will—climate control—in homes can affect the incidence of respiratory infections. Its impact on comfort and productivity in all seasons is without doubt. Health as a community resource is invaluable.

> . . . *health is, aside from the personal comfort or pain accruing to a given individual, a natural resource for the black community or any other. Health not only affects demographic composition and change; it also affects the ability of individuals—and therefore the community— to play their social, political, and economic roles. Tied in with this assumption is the fact that the advance in health since the eighteenth century may be attributed mainly to improvements in the physical environment. . . . Not only are the rates of mortality higher for blacks by each cause of death; there are some significant variations in degree. Blacks also, of course, are subject to higher rates of illness. Much of the differential causes of mortality revolve around communicable diseases, the narrowing of which has been the major factor associated with the decline in differential mortality rates by race.*

Throughout a person's life, both his probability of dying and the type of death he meets may be in large part a product of the kind of community in which he lives. It is no coincidence in this context that the high rates of death for blacks are in the area of communicable diseases and nonmotor-vehicle accidents, mainly in industry. Blacks are more than twice as likely to die from pneumonia and influenza. In the case of syphillis the death rate for blacks is about four times as high. The same is true of tuberculosis and of dysentery; and blacks die more from whooping cough and other communicable diseases. The effect of all of this for even those who do not die is relatively more activity limitations on the job than whites.

The life expectancy of blacks is almost ten years less than that of whites, and black infant and maternal mortality rates are at the level which whites exhibited twenty years ago. Black women are more than four times as likely to die of childbirth, and black children are about three times as likely to succumb to post-natal mortality. This is because (among other factors such as dietary deficiencies) black births are about twelve times as likely to occur in a setting in which there is an "attendant not in a hospital and not specified."

Moreover, poor nutrition during pregnancy and in early childhood can retard the brain's development. Illnesses and inadequate medical care combine with unsanitary conditions to effect physiological pollution. "The glazed eyes of children, legs that never grew straight, misshapen feet," and skin disorders are visible signs of this form of pollution.

Yet there is alive today a neo-Malthusian fashion which blames "population explosion" for the ecology crisis. Actually, the problem is not so much one of population explosion as population implosion, or "the increasing concentration of peoples on relatively small proportions both of the world's and America's land surface." There is both an inadequate distribution of land and people and, more significantly, of people and resources. The United States accounts for only one-fifteenth of the world's population but controls at least three-fifths of its resources. Within the United States three-fourths of the corporate wealth is controlled by about one per cent of the people. Hence one man's overpopulation is not so much a problem to him as is another man's overeating.

There is apparently something within the conditions of poverty that impels people to produce a larger number of children. Although the black birth rate is higher than that of whites, that is not true among women married to college trained men, where white women bear more children than do black women.

No solution to the ecology crisis can come without a fundamental change in the economics of America particularly with reference to blacks. Although some of the ecological differentials between blacks and whites spring directly from racism and hence defy economic correlations, many aspects of the black environmental condition are associated with basic economics. Blacks are employed in the most undesirable or polluted occupations, lagging far behind their educational attainment. About two-thirds work in unskilled and semi-skilled industries. Aggravating, and associated with, the occupational effects on the black environment is the consistently low family income of blacks which must generally support larger families. Since the turn of the century, the family income of blacks has remained about half that of whites. Six in ten of all black children must grow up in poor families. The figure is even higher for black families with a female head. Unemployment is continually at least twice as high for blacks and has been shown to affect the rate of illegitimacy and marital separation, leaving many black families fatherless.

In addition to unemployment, the same technology which defaces the general society also displaces a disproportionate number of blacks occupationally, into the throes of underemployment. At the same time, the black mother is more likely to be taken out of the home environment to work. Today the war in Vietnam continues to send many of the most vibrant black males disproportionately to die in a foreign land in battle with fellow peoples of oppression. This means that five or ten years from now, assuming that blacks do not reject monogamy, an already depleted black sex ratio will drop considerably and there will exist even a greater shortage of young black males for black women to marry. The result will be increased marital and family disorganization.

Thus the reformist solutions tendered by the current ecology movement emerge as somewhat ludicrous from the black perspective. For instance, automobiles are generally regarded to be the major source of air pollution. This is compounded in the case of blacks by the relatively smaller space in which they must live and drive amid traffic congestion and junked cars. On top of this, white commuters from the suburbs and the outer limits of the central city drive into the central city for work or recreation and social contacts, polluting the black environment further. In every region of the country there has been a direct parallel between the increase in the number of cars and the growth of the suburban and fringe population. Although automobile manufacturers are the chief profiteers, the contradiction of alien automobile polluters who daily invade and "foul the nest" of black urban residents remains.

Some of these commuters are absentee landlords who prevail as "ghetto litterbugs" by way of corrupt and negligent housing practices. Thus blacks suffer the predicament wherein the colonizer milks dry the resources and labor of the colonized to develop and improve his own habitat while leaving that of the colonized starkly "underdeveloped."

The problems of the ghetto are comparable to a colonized country. Middle city businesses and housing are owned and taxed by downtown and nothing is given in return except renewal programs that are determined by the needs of foreign interests and the transportation network that feeds downtown. . . . The job market is determined by the needs of foreign business geared to producing goods that middle city ghetto dwellers can't afford and often don't want.

The real solution to the environment crisis is the decolonization of the black race. Blacks in the United States number more than 25,000,000 people, comprising a kidnapped and captive nation surpassed in size by only twenty other nations in the entire world. It is necessary for blacks to achieve self-determination, acquiring a full black government and a multi-billion dollar budget so that blacks can better solve the more serious environmental crises of blacks. To do so blacks must challenge and confront the very foundations of American society. In so doing we shall correct that majority which appears to believe that the solution lies in decorating the earth's landscape and in shooting at the moon.

thirteen
perilous links between economic growth, justice and ecology: a challenge for economic planners

NORMAN J. FARAMELLI

Norman J. Faramelli, who was associate director, Boston Industrial Mission in Cambridge, Massachusetts, takes up the theme of social justice insisted upon by Nathan Hare. Americans have for two centuries depended upon economic growth to provide a decent life for the middle and lower levels of society. The hope has been that even those with a very small piece of the pie could look forward to more—through growth rather than through redistribution of national wealth. If this growth is to be curtailed in the name of a better environment, are we as a nation now prepared to face up to the economic meaning of the American dream of equality? And, in a larger context, Faramelli raises again the question posed by Stephen Raushenbush—What are the global implications of the assumption that the world's resources, no matter where located, exist primarily to raise the standard of living of Americans?

During 1970 the ecological crisis was brought before the American public via television, magazines, newspapers, and

Source: Norman J. Faramelli, "Perilous Links between Economic Growth, Justice and Ecology: A Challenge for Economic Planners," *Environmental Affairs* 1 (April 1971): 218–27.

other media. Despite the widespread publicity and rhetoric, the problem grows worse. The events following Earth Day (April 22), such as the summer smog along the East Coast, have offered vivid proof that our quality of life is still rapidly deteriorating.

In theory, everyone wants a clean environment. But the idea posed by *Life* magazine and others that "Ecology is everybody's issue" is misleading. There is a widespread illusion that at last we have found a real national issue that is noncontroversial, and hence, we act as if a clean environment can be obtained without cost. We forget the law of both the ecologist and the economist: "There are no free lunches"; someone will pay for environmental quality.

Environmental quality can be achieved by either expansive applications of pollution control technology, or by a long range reduction in the production of material goods. In either case there will be severe repercussions on the poor. The neglect of the poor, and the impact of specific ecology solutions on them, are among the weakest links in the ecology movement. Thus, the relationship of ecological responsibility to economic justice needs to be explored.

SHOULD ALL CONSUMERS PAY EQUALLY FOR POLLUTION CONTROL?

If the management of a chemical or power plant installs expensive pollution control equipment, it can do one of three things to cover expenditures: (1) raise the price of the product, (2) appeal for a government subsidy, or (3) reduce corporate profits. Capital expenditure in pollution control equipment is basically an investment in non-productive devices. Given our current accounting procedures, such a venture increases the cost of production. We have for years assumed that disposal of waste into the air or waterways is free. The ecological costs have seldom been calculated, let alone included in the costs of production. To do any of the three items will tend to slow down consumption and attack our cherished sacred cow—an increasing standard of living. Raising the price of a product will surely reduce the amount that a family can buy. The price increase is tantamount to a sales tax—a regressive form of taxation that hurts the poor most severely when imposed on necessities. All people pay the same amount per unit although some can afford to pay more and others cannot.

The federal subsidy also does not come free of charge, because the taxpayer will ultimately pay it, even if by a progressive income tax. Any tax credits offered to industries for cleaner effluents are really another form of subsidy for pollution control. The third alternative—lowering the corporate profits —seems unlikely, given the power, prestige of, and lack of public control over large corporations. If profits were somehow substantially reduced, however, industrial expansion would slow down and unemployment would rise. Of the three alternatives, the first seems to be the most likely. Yet increasing the price of the products—such as after-burners on automobiles, increased electric power rates, etc.—will affect the poor most severely, unless we make special allowances or adopt new pricing mechanisms.

Economic and distributive justice must be integral to all ecology debates. To have economic justice and ecological sanity we might have to revamp our pricing structures radically. For instance, we now pay less for additional units of power consumption, which means that the tenth electrical appliance is cheaper (per kilowatt hour) to operate than the first. We are enticed into consuming increasing amounts of electric power and this, in turn, increasingly contaminates the environment. In order to preserve a sound environment with economic justice, the basic units of power should be offered at the cheapest rates. Then a graduated price scale might be imposed on additional amounts so that the ninth appliance (*e.g.*, a freezer) will be more costly to operate than the first (*e.g.*, a refrigerator). The inversion of rate structures would discourage profligate use of power.

ECONOMIC GROWTH AND ENVIRONMENTAL DESTRUCTION

An increasing Gross National Product (GNP) has functioned in American society like a God concept does in a religious society. In a word, Americans worship economic growth. Yet increased economic growth which comes about by increased material and power consumption is always accompanied by increased pollution. Our perennial faith in the "technical fix" to solve all of our pollution problems is being shattered. That is, there are limits to technology; we produce new problems faster than we solve old ones. Many ecologists believe that we must begin to deal with root causes, and not symptoms. And a perpetually increasing consumption level of power and material goods, compounded by the population explosion, are the root causes.

Ecologists, who challenge the concept of perpetually increasing material economic growth, are being joined by a host of others. For instance, former Secretary of Interior Stewart Udall speaks freely of the madness involved in equating the GNP with national well-being. The geologist Preston Cloud, speaking to the last meeting of the American Association for the Advancement of Science in Boston, remarked that, "Growth is a Trojan horse, with the diplomatic privileges of a sacred cow." The biologist Rene Dubos has pointed out the insanity of such a notion as: "Produce more than you consume, so that you can consume more." There is a serious question whether ecological constraints will allow economic growth to increase indefinitely. Although the idea strikes at the heart of Keynesian economics, it is being espoused by physical, biological, and social scientists who are not known as alarmists.

Before proceeding further, it should be specified that not all economic growth results in pollution. Increased sales in pollution control equipment and gains in the "service" sector also increase the GNP. But growth in sectors that cause vast pollution should be restrained. Hence, the issue is not one of economic growth versus no growth, but what kind of economic growth.

In the short run, we can conceive of an American economy with substantially less pollution which has an even higher GNP than we now have. This can be done by curbing polluters, installing extensive pollution control equipment, and, perhaps, increasing the jobs in the public and service sectors. Of course, some polluting industries would be so taxed that they will not

survive, but other new industries will thrive. Hence, as long as we consider
the United States alone in the short run, it is conceivable that the overall
economic growth may soar while we produce considerably less pollution than
we now have. It is conceivable but, given our current economic structures
and the lack of public control over private corporations, it is not likely.
As we shall see, any optimism is short-lived when we view the
problem on a global scale.

ECONOMIC GROWTH AND EMPLOYMENT LEVELS

If it is necessary to cut back in material production, there will be serious
repercussions on the poor and lower income groups. Those who have doubts
about this should observe the rising unemployment which is a result of
our current attempt to "cool off" an inflationary economy. Also, most
industrialized nations finance their poverty programs via incremental
economic growth, or a growth dividend. A growing economy
means a bigger slice of the pie for everybody. More growth means more
jobs for all, especially the poor and lower middle income groups, and more
public funds available to finance welfare programs, without further tax
increases. In a word, we are addicted to the "trickle down theory;" *i.e.,*
everyone must receive more if the poor are to receive more. That this
theory has not been fully effective in ending poverty is irrelevant; it has not
been a total failure. The poor may not have been helped appreciably by
economic growth, but they certainly will suffer acutely if the growth rate
declines. This paradox, which can lead to a host of questions about the
structural injustices in our economic system, cannot be pursued at
this juncture.

These effects on the poor and lower middle income families are most
severe in an automated society. For years there has been a stalemate in the
debate, "Does automation produce or reduce jobs?" The experts have
argued on both sides of the issue. But from the maze of data some clear
trends are discernible. During the Eisenhower years when economic growth
was slow, unemployment rates soared (3% in 1953 to 5% in 1960).
From 1962–68, a period of economic growth, the unemployment rates dropped
from 5.6% to 3.5%. Such statistics led proautomation experts to claim that
automation produces more jobs, as long as economic growth is sustained.
But if the ecological problems are as serious as many believe, then that
provisional clause "as long as economic growth is sustained" radically alters
the debate. For automation always increases productivity, *i.e.,* units
produced per man hour. If automation did not, it would be senseless to add
new machinery. With a stagnant growth rate and increasing productivity,
the logical result must be higher levels of unemployment.

As our society becomes more industrialized, there is a shift from the
"goods" to the "service" sector. As productivity increases due to automation
more jobs will be available in the service sector. However, reliance on the
service sector to take up all of the economic slack is another myth. With a
slow industrial growth rate, the entire economy will slow down. Hence,

the problems of unemployment that will result from the slowing down of economic growth, the necessity of an adequate guaranteed annual income for all, and the need for a redistribution of national income must be included in all serious ecology debates.

A LONG-RANGE, GLOBAL VIEW

Thus far, our discussion has touched only on domestic aspects of the problem. When we consider ecology on a global basis the links between ecology and economic justice become even more pronounced. The ecological crisis is a global phenomenon; it is occurring on a planet that has a three billion year history, and, hopefully, a very long future. Hence, the problem of economic growth in the United States must be seen from a long-term, global perspective. The view presented below will be based on two premises, one from thermodynamics, and the other from social ethics:

1. The second law of thermodynamics imposes physical limitations on pollution that ever increasing material growth does not respect; and
2. Even if the United States could have an ever expanding economy with reduced pollution, there is no way to achieve it and still attain a just distribution of material and energy resources on a global basis.

1. The first argument is simple. We cannot sustain infinite material growth (with resulting pollution) in a finite biosphere. The only analogue I know of infinite growth in a fixed field is the cancer cell, and we all know what eventually happens to the fixed field. The second law of thermodynamics states that energy cannot be converted from one form to another without a heat loss; or, there is no machine that can operate at 100 percent efficiency. Stated another way, increasing energy requirements always means increasing pollution.

The problem is complicated by the compound interest law involved in economic expansion. A 4 percent per year increase in economic growth is a constant percentage of a bigger and bigger aggregate. For example, there are numerous forecasts that state that power consumption in the United States will double every ten years. As a starter, let us consider the first ten years. If the total pollution from power generating facilities is cut in half, while the total amount of power is doubled, at the end of ten years we essentially are where we started, and this means a lot of pollution. If you take the second, third, and fourth decades, the problem is enormously compounded. Even with new sophisticated pollution control devices, infinite material growth, which produces small amounts of pollution per unit of production, will eventually result in a contaminated biosphere.

Some will say that we should have faith in a "technical fix" or the dictum "technology will save us." Although there is a promising future for new recycle industries, pollution control and pollution monitoring devices,

technology has its limitations. Despite our advances in technology there seem
to be no signs that the second law will be reversed, and to believe that it
will requires more faith in technology than is warranted. Furthermore, for
those who have implicit faith in technical fixes, remember the Torrey
Canyon episode where the detergent that was used to "fix" the oil spill did
more damage to marine life than the oil.

2. If, perchance, the United States could have an expansion of material
growth without contaminating its own life support systems, the global economic
injustices would still continue and probably worsen. Hence, the issue of
economic or distributive justice is at stake. Today, the United States with
roughly 6 percent of the world's population consumes around 40–50
percent of the non-renewable resources utilized each year. According to
some estimates, by 1985 the United States will have about 5 percent of the
world's population and will consume around 55–70 percent of those
resources in order to continuously increase its "standard of living." These
figures depict a condition that is as immoral as it is insane. By any criteria
of distributive justice, to have so few people consume such a disproportionate
share is immoral. And to think that we will get away with it is insane. In
order to preserve such inequities we will need an even bigger military-
industrial complex than we now have, with massive increases in all
our violent counter-insurgency activities.

The gap between the rich and the poor nations is rapidly widening.
Increments in the United States per capita income over a two year period are
greater than the entire per capita amount in many underdeveloped nations.
It should be noted, however, that per capita income statistics do not
illustrate the disparities that still exist even in the United States. From 1967
to 1969, the per capita income in the United States rose from $3,270 to
$3,800, an increase of $530. Even discounting inflation, this increase was
about twice that of the entire per capita income in Guatemala, which
stagnated at around $250. When one considers the grossly uneven distribution
of the national income in Guatemala, that disparity is even more horrendous.
One could ask: What do Guatemalan peasants have to do with pollution
in the United States? If one tacitly sanctions the growing economic
disparities, the answer is "Nothing." That is, until a revolution brews, and
Marine battalions are dispatched to save the "free world."

We have held up to the world the American model of economic
development. The poor nations are asked to emulate us; we are the *sine qua
non* of industrial progress. With a little foreign capital, management
skills, and technology, all nations could be Americanized, so the fairy tale
goes. But that model is fraudulent. First of all, it does not seem to be
reproducible, and given the economic straight-jackets with which the rich
nations hold the poor, perpetual underdevelopment is really no big
surprise. But let us suppose that the model were reproducible, justice were
achieved, and all nations consumed and polluted at the current American
levels. If that occurred the life support systems of the planet might be
destroyed by contamination. For instance, the levels of carbon monoxide and

carbon and sulphur dioxides would increase several hundredfold. Hence, in
many ways, Americans ought to be grateful that world-wide development
has failed. Continued global poverty makes possible our over-consumption
and over-pollution.

Such alarming statements lead one to find a villain who can absorb the
full blame, particularly one external to ourselves. Some would like to blame
these problems entirely on the population explosion which is soaring
globally. It is true that population is a factor of scale, *i.e.*, whatever your
pollution problems may be, they will be so much worse with increasing
population. But even if zero population growth were in effect immediately,
the entire world's current population consuming at the present United
States level would rapidly drain global natural resources; that is, if we first
survived the increased pollution. In order to approach distributive justice
American style, the utilization of natural resources would have to
increase by factors of 10–200. Hence, in the name of global justice, the
industrialized nations should curb their profligate use of material
and energy resources.

NEW CHALLENGES

The difficulties posed by some of the suggestions offered are obvious.
First, there is the link between high employment and economic growth, or its
converse, the high unemployment that occurs during a recession. A
slowdown of economic growth would eliminate jobs primarily in the
manufacturing sector. Given our current economic arrangements, low and
moderate income families will feel the slowdown most severely. We have
received many warnings recently that the ecology issue should not be a
"cop-out" on poverty and urban problems. That advice must be seriously
heeded. Therefore, anyone in the ecology movement who advocates a
slow-down of economic growth as an answer to pollution is obligated to think
and follow through the consequences of one's proposal.

A redistribution of the national income and a refocusing of national
priorities will become imperative if economic justice is to prevail. An adequate
guaranteed annual income for all will become a necessity, and the work
force will probably have to work shorter hours. Hence, we should not entertain
the possibilities of curtailing economic growth to curb pollution until a
new kind of distribution of the national income is in effect, lest our moves
hurt the poor and lower middle income groups disproportionately. This is
the first challenge.

The second challenge is to transform the American value schema. There
will be enormous problems encountered in shifting values as we try to get
large numbers of people to live new "life-styles" which will require far less
material consumption. The American dream is rooted in a three pronged
syndrome—an active process of acquisition, consumption and disposal.
The net result of this process is dissatisfaction which we try to solve by
repeating the cycle. Hence, an insatiable material appetite makes the wheels of

American progress go around. Or, as the political philosopher Russell Baker said, "The American Dream is to convert goods into trash as fast as possible."

Our advertizing media bombard us with information which tells us that our identity depends upon our ability to buy, own, and use things; even virility is conditioned by the kind of car we drive. To talk about new "life-styles" which demand less consumption of material things gets to the roots of the American psyche. Yet new alternative life-styles are clearly needed because the present conception of the American dream is really an ecological nightmare.

The third challenge is directed to economists and others who plan economic growth. The challenge is to shift the conceptual framework of economics for developed nations from that of endless growth to a "steady state" economy for goods in the polluting sector. In this reconceptualized economy major increases will occur only in the "service" sector. A new framework should be developed which accepts the constraints of ecology and works toward global justice.

To the trained economist this proposal may seem absurd and displays a lack of understanding of the nature and function of traditional economics. Perhaps we are asking economists to go well beyond economics. Yet there is a need for reconceptualization. But we are not asking for a reversion to the stationary notions of J. S. Mill and other 19th century economists; we need a modern view which incorporates the technical innovations of our day, while taking ecology and justice seriously. The plea clearly is not for an anti-material growth model for all nations. For instance, economic growth is a necessity for under-developed nations in order to provide essential food, clothing, shelter and medical care. Hopefully, some of the new growth patterns can avoid the ecological damage of the current models.

CONCLUSION

Let us repeat the two arguments from thermodynamics and social ethics. Infinite material growth with resulting pollution in a finite biosphere will ultimately lead to disaster, unless the second law of thermodynamics is reversed. But even if technical fixes are available, economic or distributive justice cannot be a global reality as long as Americans, who desire to increase perpetually their standards of living, consume such a disproportionate amount of the world's material and energy resources.

When one explores the effects of pollution control costs on the poor, the unemployment problems that would result from a slowdown in material production, the need for new patterns of national income distributions, the lopsided distribution of wealth and income on a global basis, and the ecological limits that would prevent the entire global population from consuming at the current American level, one can truly see perilous links between economic growth, justice and ecology.

selected bibliography

Since there is no adequate history of conservation or resource policy in the United States, the story must be pieced together from specialized monographs and biographies. An asterisk indicates that the book is available in paperback.

Good background can be drawn from Leo Marx, *The Machine in the Garden: Technology and the Pastoral Ideal in America* (New York, 1964),* while Roderick Nash, in *Wilderness and the American Mind* (New Haven, 1967)* covers the full sweep of American history. Robert Shankland, in *Steve Mather and the National Parks* (New York, 1954), describes the early days of the National Park Service, and a portrait of one of Mather's most important lieutenants is drawn by Donald C. Swain in *Wilderness Defender: Horace M. Albright and Conservation* (Chicago, 1970). Roderick Nash has compiled an excellent collection, *The American Environment: Readings in the History of Conservation* (Reading, 1968).*

The Progressive conservation crusade has received the most scholarly attention of any aspect of the subject. The student should begin with J. Leonard Bates, "Fulfilling American Democracy: The Conservation Movement, 1907 to 1921," *Mississippi Valley Historical Review* 44 (June 1957), and then move to Samuel P. Hays, *Conservation and the Gospel of Efficiency: The Progressive Conservation Movement, 1890–1920* (Cambridge, 1959).* A fine account of one important event, emphasizing the divisions within the movement and the bureaucratic realities of the situation, is James Penick, Jr., *Progressive Politics and Conservation: The Ballinger-Pinchot Affair* (Chicago, 1968), and Ashley L. Schiff, *Fire and Water: Scientific Heresy in the Forest Service* (Cambridge, 1962), is a fascinating study of how research, politics, and regulation interact (in this case dealing with the problem of forest fires).

The scope of the 1920s is covered by Donald C. Swain, *Federal Conservation Policy, 1921–1933* (Berkeley, 1963), and the major controversy of those years is handled in Burl Noggle, *Teapot Dome: Oil and Politics in the 1920's* (Baton Rogue, 1962).* Various resources are the topics of Roy M. Robbins, *Our Landed Heritage: The Public Domain, 1776–1936* (Princeton, 1942); John Ise, *The United States Forest Policy* (New Haven, 1920); R. Burnell Held and Marion Clawson, *Soil Conservation in Perspective* (Baltimore, 1965); John Ise, *The United States Oil Policy* (New Haven, 1926); and James B. Trefethen, *Crusade for Wildlife: Highlights in Conservation Progress* (Harrisburg, 1961).

Arthur Maass, *Muddy Waters: The Army Engineers and the Nation's Rivers* (Cambridge, 1951), is a critical study of an agency about which conservationists had little good to say. Background on one of the New Deal's conservation efforts is offered by Preston Hubbard, *Origins of the TVA: The Muscle Shoals Controversy, 1920–1932* (Nashville, 1961), and the most famous of the conservation agencies in the 1930s is portrayed in John A. Salmond, *The Civilian Conservation Corps, 1933–1942: A New Deal Case Study* (Durham, 1967). The evolution of Roosevelt's thinking can be traced in the documents included in Edgar B. Nixon (ed.), *Franklin D. Roosevelt and Conservation, 1911–1945* (2 vols., Hyde Park, 1957).

Two classics of the immediate postwar years deserve special attention. Fairfield Osborn, *Our Plundered Planet* (Boston, 1948)* has continued to influence people with its warning against "man's conflict with nature." At about the same time, Aldo Leopold wrote *A Sand County Almanac, and Sketches Here and There* (New York, 1949).* His last section, entitled "The Land Ethic," has been particularly important in developing environmental awareness. The thinking of the 1950s has perhaps best been captured by a book sponsored by Resources for the Future, Henry Jarrett (ed.), *Perspectives on Conservation: Essays on America's Natural Resources* (Baltimore, 1958).

The key book in the revival of public interest in the environment, of course, was Rachel Carson's *Silent Spring* (Boston, 1962).* The reaction to Ms. Carson's book is told in fascinating detail in Frank Graham, Jr., *Since Silent Spring* (Boston, 1970).* A more definitive study of the problem dramatically introduced by Rachel Carson is Robert L. Rudd, *Pesticides and the Living Landscape* (Madison, 1964). One important response from the federal government was that of the President's Science Advisory Committee, *Restoring the Quality of Our Environment,* report of the Environmental Pollution Panel (Washington, 1965). An earlier report, more firmly rooted in actual government practice, was one from the Office of Science and Technology, *Research and Development on Natural Resources,* report prepared by the Committee on Natural Resources (Washington, May 1963).

The surge of concern in 1970 gave rise to a large number of books on the environment, most of them collections of essays designed to exploit or further that concern. Three national magazines devoted special issues to the problem, each of which was then turned into a book. The May 1970 issue of *Ramparts* was published as *Eco-Catastrophe* (New York, 1970);* the April 1970 issue of *The Progressive* appeared as *The Crisis of Survival* (New York, 1970);* and the February 1970 issue of *Fortune* later appeared as *The Environment: A National Mission for the Seventies* (New York, 1970).* The three emphasize, respectively, radical, liberal, and business approaches to the problem.

The national Teach-In in the spring of 1970 spawned three collections of short pieces addressing themselves to aspects of the general problem: Garrett De Bell (ed.), *The Environmental Handbook: Prepared for the First National Environmental Teach-In* (New York, 1970);* *Earth Day—The Beginning, A Guide for Survival Compiled by the National Staff of Environmental Action* (New York, 1970);* and John G. Mitchell and Constance L. Stallings (eds.), *Ecotactics: The Sierra Club Handbook for Environmental Activists* (New York, 1970).* Two other, better-focused studies appearing in 1970 are John C. Esposito, *Vanishing Air, The Ralph Nader Study Group Report on Air Pollution* (New York, 1970)* and, from the *Congressional Quarterly,* "Man's Control of the Environment"(Washington, 1970).* The latter is especially enlightening about government activities, the former about government evasions.

Two angry and radical condemnations of our environmental devastation are James Ridgeway, *The Politics of Ecology* (New York, 1970) and Gene Marine, *America the Raped: The Engineering Mentality and the Devastation of a Continent* (New York, 1969),* and a wide-ranging condemnation of the way we act is offered by novelist George R. Stewart in *Not So Rich As You Think* (Boston, 1967).* A quieter study, directed at the way laws are made and enforced, is J. Clarence Davies, III, *The Politics of Pollution* (New York, 1970),* and Lynton Keith Caldwell, *Environment: A Challenge to Modern Society* (Garden City, 1970) focuses on the policy process. Two regional studies, approaching current problems from a historical perspective, are Raymond F. Dasmann, *The Destruction of California* (New York, 1965)* and Richard G. Lillard, *Eden in Jeopardy: Man's Prodigal Meddling with His Environment, The Southern California Experience* (New York, 1966).

Collections of essays are abundant. Perhaps the best is William W. Murdoch (ed.), *Environment: Resources, Pollution and Society* (Stamford, 1971),* edited by an ecologist and containing essays both on specific resources and on general social aspects of the problem. Two volumes have come from lectures at Yale University, both edited by Harold W. Helfrich, Jr., *The Environmental Crisis: Man's Struggle to Live with Himself* (New Haven, 1970)* and *Agenda for Survival: The Environmental Crisis—2* (New Haven, 1970).* Paul Shepard and Daniel McKinley (eds.), in *The Subversive Science: Essays Toward an Ecology of Man* (Boston, 1969),* also offer a good collection of essays.

Of the books that treat particular aspects of the environmental problem, probably the most widely read is Paul R. Ehrlich, *The Population Bomb* (New York, 1968);* a broader view is taken in his more recent book, written with his wife Anne Ehrlich, *Population, Resources, Environment: Issues in Human Ecology* (San Francisco, 1970). The economic dimension was explored in Marshall I. Goldman (ed.), *Controlling Pollution: The Economics of a Cleaner America* (Englewood Cliffs, 1967);* legal avenues for reform are set forth in Malcolm F. Baldwin and James K. Page, Jr. (eds.), *Law and the Environment,* A Conference, Warrenton, Va., Sept. 1968 (New York, 1970); the role of Congress is covered in Richard A. Cooley and Goeffrey Wandesforde-Smith (eds.), *Congress and the Environment*

(Seattle, 1970); the ethical dimensions of our dealings with nature are set forth in Robert Disch (ed.), *The Ecological Conscience: Values for Survival* (Englewood Cliffs, 1970).* Finally, an authoritative attempt by scientists to measure the full dimensions of the crisis is provided in National Academy of Sciences, Committee on Resources and Man, *Resources and Man* (San Francisco, 1969).*